Finding Joy in Prayer

How to Have an Effective and Joyful Prayer Life

Connie Hubbard

CROSSBOOKS
PUBLISHING

CrossBooks™
A Division of LifeWay
1663 Liberty Drive
Bloomington, IN 47403
www.crossbooks.com
Phone: 1-866-879-0502

First published by CrossBooks 02/26/10

ISBN: 978-1-6150-7129-6 (sc)

Library Congress of Control Number: 2010920028

Printed in the United States of America
Bloomington, Indiana

This book is printed on acid-free paper.

Contents

INTRODUCTION

Much too often we view prayer as a chore instead of a privilege. We find ourselves checking it off the to-do list after a brief time of reflection. It is almost as if we don't know how to pray. We seem to dread approaching God, and when we do pray, we have difficulty knowing what to say. It does not have to be that way. And may I say that God does not want our prayer lives to be boring and dry. He is alive; therefore, our prayer lives can be filled with the joy and the life of God. Trust me, friend, there is nothing dry about being in His presence in prayer. I challenge you to test Him and see if He will not open up the windows of heaven and pour out a blessing, which will overflow from His Spirit to yours.

Many people never consider that not only does God want you to spend time talking to Him, He also wants you to spend time listening for His voice. Prayer is a two-way conversation, and it does not need to be burdensome. As a matter of fact, praying can be one of the most exciting, joyful occurrences in life. Think about it, we are talking to God. He is the most creative you can imagine. He is the most powerful you can imagine. He is the most loving you can imagine. If we could pay money to spend an hour with someone like that, most of us would sacrifice to do so. These are the things we are drawn to in a person, and yet we don't take the opportunity God gives us. Why? Could it be that we have an enemy who knows the benefits of being in God's presence? Satan tries very hard to steal God's goodness from you. Let us determine to have all the joy available to us through the privilege of prayer.

There are several key aspects to having a joyful and effective prayer life. We will touch on a few of those aspects through the course of this book. This book is meant to help you study what the Bible teaches about prayer and to help you make changes in your prayer life so that your prayers may become more effective and you might enjoy praying. As you study this book, it is my suggestion that you try to apply what you are learning in your daily prayer time.

From my experience, praise paves the way for entering God's presence and gaining His attention. When we are thankful and praise the God of heaven, the atmosphere around us changes, our perspective changes, and our desires change. As we think of and verbalize the goodness of God, our own attitude about life and all its complexities seems to change. As we are in His presence, our priorities change. Those things that we thought were of the greatest importance take a back seat to proclaiming His worth. There is absolutely nothing better than being in His presence.

Psalm 100: A Psalm of Thanksgiving

¹Shout triumphantly to the LORD, all the earth. ²Serve the LORD with gladness; come before Him with joyful songs. ³Acknowledge that the LORD is God. He made us, and we are His people, the sheep of His pasture. ⁴Enter into His gates with thanksgiving, and His courts with praise. Give thanks to Him and praise His name. ⁵For the LORD *is* good, and His love is eternal; His faithfulness endures through all generations (HCSB).

If we would only do what this one passage teaches us, our prayer lives would improve dramatically. Personally, I find singing to be a vital part of my worship experience. So often when the heavens are brass, a song sung unto the Lord will break through to beautiful sunshine, or should I say "Sonshine." To lift up my hands and my voice seems to open the windows of heaven within my soul. You do not have to sound good; I know that, because sometimes I have a hard time keeping the tune, especially when tears are flowing. You do not have to sing a complicated song. Just lift up your heart to Him, and pour out a simple song like, "Oh, How I Love Jesus" or some other simple chorus. It really does not matter what song you sing, just that your heart is touching His.

Another suggestion that Psalm 100 makes is for us to have the attitude to recognize and acknowledge who He is—God, Creator, Father, and Shepherd. Once we have that attitude, it is only natural to begin thanking Him. Thanking Him for what He has done leads us right into praising Him for who He is, recognizing and acknowledging His character. Once we enter into praise, we freely bless His name.

But You *are* Holy, enthroned on the praises of Israel. (Psalms 22:3, HCSB)

This psalm teaches us that God inhabits the praises of His people. As we are in His presence, we know beyond all things that He is good. We become aware of His mercy and His truth. We begin to see things differently once we are aware of being in His presence.

My favorite song at this time in my life is "In The Presence of Jehovah"_(by Geron and Becky Davis [1985], Meadowgreen Music/Songchannel Music Company [all rights administered by EMI CMG Publishing]). The chorus says, "In the presence of Jehovah, God Almighty, Prince of Peace, troubles vanish; hearts are mended, in the presence of the King." No truer song has ever been written. When we are in God's presence, things just look different. Only in the presence of Jehovah can hearts be mended. Only the Prince of Peace makes troubles vanish. When we stand in His presence, the only thing that matters is Him, loving Him. If you have ever been there, you know exactly what I mean. You have never really known the joy of being in His presence until you feel like you are standing face to face with Him. I pray that you will learn to come into His presence through the wonderful privilege of prayer. May God grant your heart's desire to know Him more completely through the study of His word and through personal prayer.

Matthew 6:9–13

⁹Therefore, you should pray like this: Our Father in heaven, Your name be honored as holy. ¹⁰Your kingdom come. Your will be done on earth as it is in heaven. ¹¹Give

us today our daily bread. ¹²And forgive us our debts, as we also have forgiven our debtors. ¹³And do not bring us into temptation, but deliver us from the evil one. For Yours is the kingdom and the power and the glory forever. Amen (HCSB).

The springboard for this study will be the prayer that the Lord prayed in Matthew 6:9–13. When Jesus's disciples asked about how to pray, Jesus gave them, and us, this passage as a model prayer. Jesus was pretty straightforward in most of His responses; therefore, it is safe to assume that much of what we need to know about praying can be found in this passage.

This will not be an exhaustive study of this particular passage. It is my prayer that this study will lay a foundation that you will be able to build on for years to come. Will you join me in a prayer, as we begin this journey together?

Heavenly Father, I pray for each person participating in this study who has a desire to go deeper with You. I pray that each person would come to know You in much greater intimacy by the time they complete this study. I pray also for the one who is unsure about even wanting to know You in deep intimacy. I ask that You calm their fear and assure them that where You are there is goodness and peace.

Father, as each person endeavors to go deeper with You, may they be blessed with the knowledge of Your will in their lives. May they have an ever-increasing longing to be with You and to love You. I pray each person would be willing to spend whatever time is needed to get to know You through prayer. Lord, may You open their eyes and hearts to hear You and to see You in their daily lives. I pray that they would have an expectant heart, believing You are willing to reveal Yourself to them as they seek Your face. I pray each person will have a heart turned toward You. Lord, teach them how to meet with You consistently in prayer. Teach them how to pray in a way that is pleasing to You. Teach each of them how to have a joyful and effective prayer life. Amen.

Each week you will have a chapter about a different prayer principle. Each prayer principle will be about a different aspect of prayer, some things that might help you to deepen your prayer life. After each chapter, you will be given five short daily devotional studies. You will be asked to read one devotional for each of the five days following each chapter. Please do not skip over the daily devotionals. They may be the most important part of this book. They are designed as a means of application related to the principle just studied. On the sixth and seventh days, you may use any or all of the previous devotionals in your prayer time, or you may choose to add your own deeper understanding of what God is doing in your life personally. Be assured that God is at work in your life. He is working His purpose within you. Yield to Him. He is good. Ask Him to reveal a new truth to you each day.

All Scripture passages used in this book will be from the *New King James Version, New American Standard Bible* or *Holman Christian Standard Bible* unless otherwise stated. Definitions used in this book are taken from *The Complete Word Study Dictionary, Old and New Testaments* (AMG Publishers, 6815 Shallowford Road, Chattanooga, Tenn. 37421, 2003 & 1992).

SUGGESTIONS FOR USING THIS BOOK

It is not my intent to tell anyone how to pray. It is, however, my hope that those individuals who want a deeper, joyful, and effective prayer life will read this book with an open mind and heart. As you read, you may think the principles are too simple or the devotionals too intruding. It is my prayer that you will find the material in this book gets to the heart of the matter—your heart.

I pray you use this book as a personal study first and then, if you want, use it as a means of teaching others how to develop personal joy in praying. I challenge you to do each thing suggested as much as possible. You may not be accustomed to some of the suggestions, but I encourage you to do them anyway. If you are serious about a deeper prayer life, I urge you to complete the exercises. Of course, use your own judgment. I do, however, ask that you commit to stretching yourself spiritually, even if it means going beyond your comfort zone temporarily.

I suggest that you determine before God to complete this book and the suggestions found within it. If after you have completed this book and you have greater joy in prayer, all I ask is that you give testimony of God's goodness within your local church.

Within each devotional, you will find a directive to prepare yourself for prayer. During the first few devotionals, I will give specific directives as to how you might prepare yourself. Even those days that I do not specifically direct you, please remember to do those things previously taught. The goal is to quiet our hearts before Him and to praise Him as we enter His presence. It is good when we become aware of the fact that we have come before His presence and are ready to communicate with Holy God. As you begin to experience His presence, you will know when you have prepared your heart for prayer.

On several occasions, you will be asked to, "pray a Scripture back to God." Maybe you have never done that before. If not, you will find it one of the greatest blessings of praying. The Word of God is powerful and active. The Word of God is alive. For those who are new to this practice, let me demonstrate. Let's take John 3:16 as an example: "For God loved the world in this way: He gave His One and Only Son, so that everyone who believes in Him will not perish but have eternal life" (John 3:16) (HCSB).

If I was praying this Scripture, I might pray something like this, "Father, I thank You that You loved me so much that You sent Jesus to die for my sins. Thank You, Lord, that Jesus was willing to take up the cross and pay for all the sins I have committed. Thank You, Lord, that I will never have to perish because of what You did for me. Thank You, Father, that I will never have to be separated from You. I cannot imagine what it must have been like to watch Your only begotten Son in such agony. I am so glad that You loved me and all who would come so much that You were willing to pay the price for my sins. I am forever grateful. I gladly give my life to You in service. I praise You for Your great love. Thank You that Your love extends to the whosoever and right now I pray for _____, that they would come to understand such a great love and price paid for their sins."

Look at every aspect of the Scripture and either praise God for the truth of it or use it in petition. Be as detailed as you like.

I would also suggest that, as much as possible, you read aloud the Scripture given for each devotional. Again, the Word of God is alive and active, and saying it makes it more real to you. Speaking the truth allows you not only to say it but you also hear it. By speaking Scripture, you see, hear, and speak it. You get as much impact as possible, and it is much harder for your mind to wander.

Be blessed by the mighty hand of God, as you make your joyful prayer journey over the next weeks.

Amazed by His Grace
Connie Hubbard.

CHAPTER 1

God: The Object of Our Prayers

Is God really able to do anything? Is He able to move in my situation? Does God really care about my situation? Maybe these are questions you have asked yourself. Let's see what we can find out about God and find the answers to these questions and more.

Psalm 148:13

¹³Let them praise the name of the LORD, for His name alone is exalted. His majesty covers heaven and earth (HCSB).

Who is this God that we pray to? There is no one name that can contain the greatness of God. His majesty covers the earth and heaven! Elohim is the name first used for God in the Old Testament (OT). "In the beginning God created the heavens and the earth" (Genesis 1:1) (HCSB). Elohim indicates His power and preeminence, His greatness and majesty, His creative power, His glory. *El* is translated mighty, strong, and prominent. Elohim is able to speak life into existence. This name describes the God of heaven, who stepped out in His great power and said, "Let there be light," and there was light. Every day since then, there has been light.

God is also revealed as God Almighty. He is the one who is able to perform whatever He wants. In the New Testament (NT), Elohim-God is translated "Theos," which indicates the one true God. In the beginning, God was there, and at the end of Scripture God is there: He is eternal.

The name Elohim also bears the idea of a covenant relationship. Think of a marriage relationship: what affects your spouse also affects you. Our relationship with God is a covenant relationship and what affects us cannot be separated from the covenant partner. When someone hurts you, it is also directed toward your covenant partner. You have His strength and power available to you. He cares about what you care about. Do you care about the things God cares about? His strength is your strength. Do you rely on His strength or your own? Are you a reliable covenant partner to God?

God is omnipotent and the Creator and Ruler of the universe, and He has absolute authority. God is able to do anything and everything about the situation that we bring to Him in prayer. We pray to the God who spoke, and the world was created! How awesome that is! If we are in a covenant relationship with God, our enemies are His enemies, and His enemies should be our enemies. Do you live as if they are, or do you regularly entertain them as welcome guests in your life?

Another name used for God in the Scriptures is Jehovah. (When LORD with all capitals is used it is referring to the name Jehovah). "These are the records of the heavens and the earth, concerning their creation at the time that the LORD God made the earth and the heavens" (Genesis 2:4) (HCSB). He is righteous and holy. Jehovah indicates His unoriginated (has no beginning), immutable (cannot change), eternal, self-sustaining (needs nothing or no one to keep Him alive), and permanent existence. He has no beginning, He cannot change, and He needs nothing or no one to keep Him alive.

We are totally dependent on Him for our existence. We do not have life within ourselves. There is absolutely nothing that I can do to make myself breathe the next breath. There is nothing that I can do to make my heart beat the next beat. If you don't believe me, go ahead try to make your own heart beat. I, as well as you, am totally dependent on Him for life. He is the only One who is self-existent, because He is the source of all life.

When God wanted to reveal Himself in a special way, He used the name Jehovah. When God chose to reveal certain characteristics of Himself, He used compound names. Jehovah-jireh is one example. God is saying, "I am the LORD and this is what I can do—provide."

God is also known as the Holy One of Israel. "For the Lord God, the Holy One of Israel, has said: 'You will be delivered by returning and resting; Your strength will lie in quiet confidence.' But you are not willing" (Isaiah 30:15); "But as He who called you is holy, you also are to be holy in all your conduct" (1 Peter 1:15) (HCSB). God is holy. He is a Holy God, who is totally separated, completely untouched by evil. He is the opposite of that which is common.

Psalms 33:8–9

⁸Let the whole earth tremble before the LORD; let all the inhabitants of the world stand in awe of Him. ⁹For He spoke, and it came into being; He commanded, and it came into existence (HCSB).

How are we to view this God that we pray to? We should view God with awe, with reverence, and with respect. One hindrance to a joyful and effective prayer life is a lack of reverence for God.

When the priests in the OT entered the Holy of Holies, they had to be sinless, or else they would die as they came before His presence. They had such reverence for God they would not write or speak His name casually. Do we view God in such a manner? Do we really believe that He is holy? Our actions and our words are a reflection of what is in our hearts. Do our actions and words show those around us that God is in our hearts?

Sometimes people live in such a way as to see how close we can get to breaking God's laws without actually sinning. For example, we may flirt, we may play with lust, we may allow certain sexual activities—getting as close to adultery as possible without actually completing a sexual experience. We can deceive ourselves into believing that as long as we did not cross a particular line, we are okay. Instead, if our heart's desire is to please God instead of pleasing our flesh, we should be thinking about how we can stay away from sin.

On the other hand the Pharisees became too strict in their interpretation of the law, but their original motivation was to establish laws that would ensure they never reached a point of breaking the law of God. The problem is when we try to do anything in our own strength, we either fail miserably, or it becomes a point of pride, as it did with many of the Pharisees. Our goal is to walk by the Spirit, not by the flesh. God's promise is that with every temptation, He will provide a way of escape. Read 1 Corinthians 10:13.

> **Isaiah 40:25 (HCSB)**
>
> 25 **Who will you compare Me to, or who is My equal?" asks the Holy One.**
>
> **Isaiah 57:15 (HCSB)**
>
> 15 **For the High and Exalted One who lives forever, whose name is Holy says this: "I live in a high and holy place, and with the oppressed and lowly of spirit, to revive the spirit of the lowly, and to revive the heart of the oppressed."**

How do you treat His name? For our prayer lives to be joyful and effective we must honor His name and remember who it is that we are addressing in prayer. We learned from the model prayer in Matthew 6:9 that we are to hallow His name. We must honor His name as holy.

According to the *Key Word Study Bible Lexical Aid*, the word "hallowed" means to sanctify, and it is in contrast to being defiled or common. It can also be used as to make or set apart as Holy, to respect or honor greatly; to revere. The word "holy" means to be associated with a divine power; sacred; worthy of awe; revered; spiritually pure. Personally, I only use the word "awesome" when referring to the only one worthy of awe: God.

God is Holy; His name is Holy. We have made His name commonplace in most things that we do. In our homes, in our relationships, and at our workplaces, His name isn't hallowed or made holy. We have lost the awe of God. We have lost a great deal of respect for who God really is, His name as well as His power.

1 Samuel 2:2 (HCSB)

² **There is no one holy like the LORD. There is no one besides You. And there is no rock like our God.**

The word "common" means that which is ordinary or that which we treat with little value. Many of us have made God common in our lives. We use God's name in a common way even within our churches. How often have you heard someone, or you yourself, say, "God bless you"? Do we actually stop and think about the God we just addressed, or is it something that we say without really thinking about Him? People use the name of Jesus as a byword and never stop to consider the implications of making His name as common as the refuse on the bottom of our shoes.

Other people use the name of God in an attempt to make a point of anger, not realizing that in Exodus 20:7, God states that the one who uses His name in vain will not go unpunished. Then there are those who have made a habit of using the Lord's name in vain. The ancient Hebrew people would not even speak His name for fear of taking it in vain, and now His name has become so commonplace that it is used as a habit of life. My heart grieves at the thought.

God's house should also be respected, because it is a place set aside to worship the Most Holy God. Today, God's house has become a game room. It is a place of entertainment, a place used to accommodate anyone who is perceived as a seeker. It is a place built and used more for the comfort and consideration of the people who occasionally attend than for the God who can actually give them what they are seeking. His name is used as slang. His Word is no longer considered truth. His commands are now said to be relative. God has become common to us in our lives and in our worship.

Until we revere God, we will not have an effective prayer life; neither will we have joy in praying. Let's seek to regain our awe for God. Let's teach our children to revere and respect God. When they respect God, they will respect His house; it will be an automatic overflow of our heart. God needs to be treated differently, because He is different. There is no one else like Him. He is not common; there is no Rock like our God.

When we pray, we need to remember whom we are addressing in prayer—a Holy, living God. He is God Almighty, Creator of the universe, Lord of Lords, and King of Kings! He is God! When you pray, imagine that you are before His throne. When we bow on our knees in prayer, we must remember and become aware that we are addressing the one true Holy God. If we treat Him casually, He will not respond to us in the manner we want. We are not bowing before a friend; we are bowing before God.

In order to have an effective and joyful prayer life, we must first do three things. First, we have to regain awe and reverence for God. Second, we have to stop making God, His name, His Word, and His worship commonplace. Third, we must see Him as the Holy God, worthy of our reverence.

GOD: THE OBJECT OF OUR PRAYERS

Devotionals

God: The Object of Our Prayers

He Is Holy

Isaiah 6:1–3 (NKJV)

¹In the year that King Uzziah died, I saw the Lord sitting on a throne, high and lifted up, and the train of His *robe* filled the temple. ²Above it stood seraphim: each one had six wings; with twain he covered his face, with twain he covered his feet, and with twain he did fly. ³And one cried to another and said: "Holy, holy, holy is the LORD of hosts; the whole earth is full of His glory!"

This Scripture gives us a picture of what might be going on in heaven right now. Seraphim crying, one to another, "Holy, holy, holy is the LORD of hosts; the whole earth is full of His glory!" If I understand correctly, to say the word "holy" twice in Hebrew is to describe someone as "most holy." To say the word "holy" three times intensifies the idea to the highest level. In other words, the holiness of God is indescribable in human language. Yet, the whole earth is full of His glory. Pretty incredible isn't it? God, whose holiness is so indescribable, still reaches down in His mercy to take care of us.

According to the *Key Word Study Bible Dictionary*, the word "holy" (*qadosh*) means that because God is holy, He is completely free from moral imperfections and failures associated with mankind. He is incapable of being touched by all the imperfections that we are plagued with, all those things that make us feel bad toward ourselves and others. I do not mean that God is not touched with the feeling of our infirmities; He is. It is that He is free from the influences of evil or sin. I do not know about you, but this is a hard concept for me to grasp. But I am so thankful that it is true.

Again according to the *Key Word Study Bible Dictionary*, the basic meaning of the word "holy" is that which is intrinsically sacred and distinct, even opposed to what is common. He is not thought of or spoken of as others would be. He is separate, He is pure. There is no other who can claim complete purity.

What does it mean for you that our God is holy? It means that He is totally pure. Every thought toward you is pure. Every feeling toward you is without the influence of evil; His thoughts are pure, holy, and right. Every act toward you is right. He has a pure, holy love for you that we mortals cannot fully comprehend. Because He is holy, we can depend on Him to be absolutely faithful to His promises. Because He is holy, He cannot lie. Because He is holy, He does, and is, only good. Because He is holy, we can trust Him completely.

Would you join those in heaven proclaiming His holiness? Would you right now also declare His holiness? I challenge you to get alone with God in a place of privacy. Get on your knees before the Lord of hosts and declare His holiness. Begin by saying to Him, "Holy, holy, holy, are you, Oh Lord." Just cry, "Holy" unto the Lord until you begin to feel His holiness, to see and understand His holiness within your spiritual being.

As you go into your prayer closet and get on your knees, I want to make some prayer suggestions. Picture yourself alone, bowing before the King of Kings. It is just you before Holy God. Begin to think about what it means that the God you serve is holy, and He is your Father.

Begin your prayer time by:

- Joining in the cry of heaven by proclaiming His holiness. "Holy, Holy, Holy, is the Lord God Almighty. The whole earth is full of His glory!" Just repeat "Holy, Holy, Holy, are You, Lord God Almighty." Think of His purity, His righteousness. Declare His righteousness. You may feel silly saying this out loud, but continue anyway. Declare His holiness. Say it until something changes within you, until you mean it with all your heart. Praise Him for His holiness.

- Praise Him that He is free from moral impurities and failures. Praise Him that He cannot be touched by evil, that He is far removed from it. Ask Him to point out your moral imperfections and to forgive you for them, if He brings anything to mind. Ask Him to keep you from evil.

- Praise Him that He is sacred and distinct. Praise Him that He is opposed to what is common, that He is separate, cut off from the impurity of the world. Ask Him to reveal any way you make Him or His name common. Ask Him to help you keep Him in His rightful place in your life. Ask Him to reveal any way you make His house or His Word commonplace in your life. Ask Him to give you an awe and reverence for Him, His name, His house, and His Word.

- Praise Him that He is faithful to keep His promises and that it is impossible for Him to lie. Praise Him that you can always trust Him. Ask Him to show you areas in your life where you are not faithful to Him. Repent as He leads, and praise Him for His forgiveness.

- Tell Him that you love Him and want to learn how to love Him more.

- As I was writing this devotional, I got up before daybreak, got on my knees, and began crying, "Holy, Holy, Holy is the Lord of Host," the same thing I am asking of you. As I began feeling His response to my praise, I wanted to sing to Him. I began singing this old song to Him. It was a blessing to me, and I pray that it will be to you also. If you know it, sing it to Him. If you don't, read the words and praise Him.

"Holy, Holy, Holy"

Holy, Holy, Holy: Lord God Almighty.
Early in the morning, our song shall rise to thee.
Holy, Holy, Holy! Merciful and mighty!
God in Three Persons, blessed Trinity.
Holy, Holy, Holy: all the saints adore Thee.
Casting down their golden crowns around the glassy sea.
Cherubim and Seraphim, falling down before Thee,
Which wert and art, and evermore shall be.
Holy, Holy, Holy: Lord God Almighty.
All thy works shall praise Thy name in earth and sky and sea.
Holy, Holy, Holy! Merciful and mighty!
God in Three Persons, blessed Trinity!

God: The Object of Our Prayers

Jehovah-jireh: The Lord Will Provide

Genesis 22:1–14 (HCSB)

¹After these things God tested Abraham, and said to him, "Abraham!" And he said, "Here, I am." ² "Take your son," He said, "your only son Isaac, whom you love, go to the land of Moriah, and offer him there as a burnt offering on one of the mountains I will tell you about." ³So early in the morning Abraham got up, saddled his donkey, and took with him two of his young men and his son Isaac. He split wood for a burnt offering and set out to go to the place God had told him about. ⁴On the third day Abraham looked up and saw the place in the distance. ⁵Then Abraham said to his young men, "Stay here with the donkey. The boy and I will go over there to worship; then we'll come back to you." ⁶Abraham took the wood for the burnt offering and laid *it* on Isaac his son. In His hand he took the fire and the sacrificial knife, and the two of them walked on together. ⁷Then Isaac spoke to Abraham his father and said, "My father!" And he replied, "Here I am, my son." Isaac said, "The fire and the wood are here but where is the lamb for a burnt offering?" ⁸Abraham answered, God Himself will provide the lamb for a burnt offering, my son." Then the two of them walked on together. ⁹When they arrived at the place that God had told them about, Abraham built the altar there and arranged the wood. He bound his son Isaac and placed him on the altar, on top of the wood. ¹⁰Then Abraham reached out his hand and took the knife to slaughter his son. ¹¹But the Angel of the LORD called to him from heaven and said, "Abraham, Abraham!" He replied, "Here I am." ¹²Then He said, "Do not lay a hand on the boy, or do anything to him. For now I know that

you fear God, since you have not withheld your son, your only son, from Me." ¹³Abraham looked up and saw a ram caught by its horns in the thicket. So Abraham went and took the ram and offered it as a burnt offering in place of his son. ¹⁴And Abraham called the name of the place The LORD Will Provide (Jehovah-jireh), so today it is said; "It will be provided on the LORD'S mountain."

This Scripture is a wonderful a picture of what was to come through God's provision of the supreme sacrifice—Jesus. How many times has God spoken something to you, and since you could not *see* how He would bring it about, you questioned your accuracy in hearing His words? Or maybe you questioned His ability to perform great and mighty things.

The promise was given—Abraham would become the father of a great nation, and now God was asking him to sacrifice his only son. How could this be? I can imagine the thoughts that must have been going through Abraham's mind, as he and the boy climbed that steep mountain. "Did I hear God right? I'm just a man. Could I have made a huge mistake? Could this be the enemy trying to destroy God's promise to me?" Maybe Abraham did not ask himself all of these questions, but I sure would have.

When Abraham pulled back his arm to kill his son, it looked to the outside world like the promise was over. But Abraham believed that God would raise his son from the dead if need be. Abraham believed God! When Jesus hung on the cross, his disciples must have thought that they, too, had believed a lie. They thought their dreams and hopes for the future kingdom on earth had just breathed its dying breath.

What God speaks to us may be as simple as urging us to testify of His greatness, or sing a song, or teach a lesson. We question His ability or faithfulness to provide what we need as we need it. Maybe the Lord has placed some great desire within you, but you think it must be your own idea. God could not work such a thing through you. Maybe He could work through someone else but not through you.

Let me assure you, God will provide what He promises. It probably will not be in the way you expect, just as Jesus's death, burial, and resurrection were not how the disciples had it figured. God will bring your plans to a place of death so that He can resurrect His plans through you. I don't know if you have ever noticed, but God often allows it to appear that the Word He has given us dies just before He produces life in another area or way. To our amazement, the promise He gave has been completed. Only this time, we know for sure it was all His doing. We would never have thought to do it that way. God is *good*!

Ephesians 1:3–7 (NKJV)

³Blessed *be* the God and Father of our Lord Jesus Christ, who has blessed us with every spiritual blessing in the heavenly *places* in Christ, ⁴just as He chose us in Him before the foundation of the world, that we should be holy and without blame before Him in love, ⁵having predestined us to adoption as sons by Jesus Christ to Himself, according to the good pleasure of His will, ⁶to the praise of the glory of His grace, by which He made us accepted in the Beloved.

⁷In Him we have redemption through His blood, the forgiveness of sins, according to the riches of His grace …

This passage tells us that He chose us in Him before the foundation of the world. God chose you, precious one, to be His. This Scripture is not teaching that some are chosen for salvation and others cannot be saved. Do not get hung up on that! According to 2 Peter 3:9, "God is long suffering toward us, not willing that *any* should perish, but that *all* should come to repentance."

As you prepare to pray today and each day get alone and quiet before God. Do all the things you have learned thus far; bow before Him if you can, imagine you are knelling before His throne, and revere Him as you acknowledge His holiness. Remember, it is God you are praying to.

Thank and praise God of heaven for being the Lord who will provide. Praise Him that He is the Father of our Lord Jesus Christ. Before the foundation of the world, He gave Jesus Christ as the supreme sacrifice for your sin and mine. Thank Him that He has blessed you with every spiritual blessing in heavenly places in Jesus Christ. You don't have to know all of what it means about spiritual blessings in heavenly places. Just thank Him anyway. Continue through the passage praying the

Scripture back to Him, thanking Him for all it says He has given to you. Praise Him that He has made you accepted in the Beloved, Jesus Christ.

God has provided so many things that we never even realize He's provided. About ten to twelve years ago, I sat down to eat my lunch at the parsonage beside our church. My husband is the pastor. I was alone, and as I bowed my head to thank God for the provision of the food and water I was about to have, God opened my eyes to see how He had provided for me long before I was born. He showed me how He planned the water moving through the earth as provision for His people. I understood how, in creation, He provided food for us to eat, provision that would continue throughout the course of time. He did not just throw this world into being without thought of you and me and what we would need today. The Lord's presence filled me that day, and I praised Him for His provision at a depth I had never known before. God is so *good!*

As you pray today:

- Think about how the Lord has provided for you. In the passage from Genesis, you read that God is described as Jehovah-jireh, the Lord will provide. Ask God to open your eyes to how He provided for you through Jesus. Revelation 13:8 tells us that Christ was slain from the foundation of the world. This means that before the world was formed God had already provided a sacrifice for us. He did not create us without hope of redemption. He provided long before we were ever created. God's provision was not just some small something; it was His only Begotten Son.

- Thank Him for His provision of Jesus Christ. Thank Him that He provided someone to tell you about His saving power. Thank Him specifically for that person or persons. Thank Him for providing conviction and leading you to repentance. Thank Him for providing salvation. These are not small things, but we often take them for granted and fail to remember His goodness and mercy toward us.

- Make a list of things He has provided in your life and then thank Him for each one of them.

- Thank Him that He is Jehovah-jireh, the Lord will provide. That means in whatever you face in the future, you belong to the Lord, who will provide. He will provide the thing you need when it is needed. Thank Him that He is not only able but willing to provide your every need. Read Psalm 37:25 and thank Him that you will never be forsaken. He will always provide! Praise His wonderful name!

God: The Object of Our Prayers

Jehovah-rophe: The Lord, Your Healer

Exodus 15:22–26 (HCSB)

²²Then Moses led Israel on from the Red Sea, and they went out to the Wilderness of Shur. They journeyed for three days in the wilderness without founding water. ²³ They came to Marah, but they could not drink the water at Marah because it was bitter-that is why it was named Marah. ²⁴The people grumbled to Moses, "what are we going to drink?" ²⁵So he cried out to the LORD, and the LORD showed him a tree. When he threw it into the water, the water became drinkable. He made a statute and an ordinance for them at Marah and He tested them there, ²⁶He said, "If you will carefully obey the LORD your God, and do what is right in His eyes, pay attention to His commands, and keep all His statutes, I will not inflict any illness on you I inflicted on the Egyptians. For I *am* the LORD who heals you."

Moses had just led the children of Israel out of Egypt. They had crossed the Red Sea on dry land. They went three days into the wilderness and became thirsty, but there was no water to be found. They had already come out of bondage—a type of salvation. They were only three days away from the Lord's deliverance when they became thirsty again. To me, that is a picture of how short a walk it is away from God's deliverance into our own need. If we go away from His deliverance, our need becomes evident once again.

When the Israelites found the waters of Marah, the water was bitter. Again, this to me is a picture of how, when we try to meet our own needs, we always wind up with bitter water. If we are not careful, we allow bitter water to make us bitter. The children of Israel complained, asking, "What shall we drink?" They cried out to the wrong provider. Thank God, Moses cried out to the One who could reveal truth.

God showed Moses a tree to throw into the water. As he was obedient, the waters became sweet, and the people were able to drink and be satisfied. Obedience is sweet, and it will satisfy.

In verse 26, God says He is the Lord, your healer. He also says His people should be careful to obey His voice, to do what is right, and keep His commands. If His people were obedient in those ways, He would not need to discipline them. They would remain in His protection. Please hear me clearly: I am not suggesting that all sickness and disease is a result of our disobedience. That is just not true.

Job was an example, and even Paul was an example of men whose illnesses had nothing to do with their disobedience. We do not understand all the ways of the Lord. Just let it be established, that Scripture teaches Jehovah-rophe is the Lord your healer. This Scripture does not mean that every sickness will be healed on this earth, nor does it mean God is displeased with you if you are not healed in the here and now. As Isaiah 55:8–9 teaches, His ways are higher than ours.

What has He healed? First, the tree Moses threw into the water could represent the Savior's tree. I think in a sense that it does, but I think it is broader than the cross at Calvary. Many years ago, while studying this Scripture, the Lord opened my eyes to the fact that the tree was there long before the need was present. It just took the Lord pointing out to Moses and directing him to throw it into the water. The thing that was needed to change their situation was in their midst, only they were not aware of it. God had to point it out for it to be effective.

How do I see God as our healer? First and foremost, God is a healer of our sin problem through salvation. In addition, He created our bodies in such a way that we have the ability to fight sickness and disease. Our bodies can recover from incredible problems. I believe God can and does miraculously heal the most dreaded of diseases as He chooses, and yes, in our day. He is able!

I also believe God heals our emotional ills. I have seen far more people crippled by some past emotional pain than I have ever seen in wheelchairs. Far more people have been blinded by some abuse or some unmet need than those whose eyes cannot see the light of day.

There are broken, blind, and lame people walking around us every day who need Jehovah-rophe to act on their behalf to heal their emotional sicknesses. Trust me, He can do that, and He wants to do that.

Years ago, before I was a counselor, I was in so much pain I fell on my knees and cried out to the Lord for help. I often felt a rage I did not understand, and it sometimes scared me. One day after becoming so angry I wanted to hit someone, I cried out to God to free me from this rage. There, in the middle of the living room floor, God took me back in my mind and heart to a time when I was five years old. He revealed the pain and fear I experienced that day and showed me how it was connected to what I was presently feeling.

Through revealing that truth, God began the process of healing the hurt that caused such rage within me. I sat on the floor that day, sobbing, and in my mind, comforting a five-year-old, frightened child. Through the years, many such times have occurred in my life. I am still a long way from complete healing, but I am much closer than I once was. I know that when I begin experiencing feelings that are contrary to His word and His ways, it is an open window for me to run to the Healer.

As you begin your prayer time today, thank God that He is your Healer. Please remember, He has always been there to heal you. He is in your midst, just as the tree at Marah. What bitter waters within you need to be healed? What past hurt or rejection have you allowed to make you bitter? You just need to become aware of how He can change the bitter circumstances of your life to the sweet fragrance of His nature. *He is very good!*

As you go to Him in prayer today, kneel before Him and with a grateful heart:

- Thank Him that He healed your sin sickness, without which you would be bound for hell. Without salvation, you would not have the indwelling power of the Holy Spirit. Thank Him for each of these things.

- Thank Him that He made your body in such a way as to heal itself of many things, things we may never know about.

- He can and does miraculously heal. Maybe He has healed you in that way. Praise His name.

- He wants to heal your emotional pain. Ask the Lord to show you if there is something He wants to heal in you right now. Trust Him. He will not lead you anywhere He is not able to keep you safe. Ask Him if there is bitterness within you that He wants to heal.

- Thank Him that He will always be the same. He will always be available as your Healer.

God: The Object of Our Prayers

Jehovah-rohi: The Lord, Your Shepherd

Psalm 23 (NKJV)

¹The LORD *is* my shepherd; I shall not want. ²He makes me to lie down in green pastures; He leads me beside the still waters. ³He restores my soul; He leads me in the paths of righteousness for His name's sake. ⁴Yea, though I walk through the valley of the shadow of death, I will fear no evil; for You are with me; Your rod and Your staff, they comfort me. ⁵You prepare a table before me in the presence of my enemies; You anoint my head with oil; my cup runs over. ⁶Surely goodness and mercy shall follow me all the days of my life; and I will dwell in the house of the LORD forever.

Please get your Bible and read John 10:3–5, 11, 15, 27–29.

This name for our God is probably the one that expresses His intimacy with us, His sheep. The shepherd lives with the sheep day and night. Jesus explained in John 10 that the sheep know His voice. He leads them with His voice. He calls each by name. He protects the sheep from all kinds of harm. He provides pasture and water. He goes after the lost ones and carries them on His shoulders, returning them to safety. He will bind up the wounded. He is so devoted to the sheep that He lays down His life for them. He lies down as the door to the sheepfold as their protection at night. Nothing can enter or exit without going over Him first.

Jehovah-rohi offers that kind of intimate relationship to us, His sheep. Sheep will go astray without the presence of their shepherd. Sheep are dumb, helpless animals. Read Ezekiel 34:11–16. This passage paints a picture of one who pursues the sheep, searching for them, seeking them out to feed and protect them, to provide for them.

Jesus qualified Himself to be the Good Shepherd. He became a lamb that He might understand the needs and fears of being a defenseless sheep. He was the Lamb led to slaughter. Jesus often referred to Himself as the Shepherd and His people as sheep. He was not insulting us. He was showing the tenderness He felt toward us and the intimacy He pledges to us.

Do you know His voice? Have you spent enough time in His presence to recognize His familiar tone? Have you felt His touch often enough to trust it? Do you know the Lord as *your* Shepherd? If He is your Shepherd, do you recognize that your welfare depends completely on the care of the Shepherd? Our Shepherd is a Sovereign God. Nothing happens without His approval. He declares that He is the Good Shepherd. Whatever He allows is ultimately good for you.

The *Hebrew Key Study Bible* states that the primary meaning of the word "*ro'eh*" is to feed or lead to pasture, as a shepherd does his flock. A further definition relates to "compassion" or "friend," expressing the idea of the intimacy of sharing life and food. It is the word used for friend in Exodus 33:11, when God spoke to Moses face to face, as a man speaks to his friend. It also relates to things like, cherish, take pleasure in, or something treasured. This definition shows the intimate nature of the relationship a shepherd has with his sheep. It portrays a tender, loving relationship.

As you prepare to pray today, do all of the things you have learned thus far. Get alone with Him and acknowledge His goodness.

- Although we will not study each section of Psalm 23, I suggest that you pray each section back to God in thanksgiving. Suffice it to say that sheep cannot live without pasture and water. Sheep are afraid of swift waters. They can be swept away easily for several reasons. Notice the Shepherd leads them to still waters.

- Again, I ask you, do you know Him intimately? Do you know His voice? Do you trust Him to care for you? Are you willing to follow where He leads? Would you be willing to ask yourself each of these questions as you go before God's spotlight in prayer? If you cannot answer these questions in the affirmative, I pray that you would ask God to increase your desire to know Him intimately, to know His voice, to be willing to follow

Him. Are you ready to follow your Shepherd? Oh, beloved, I pray that you are.

- Remember God, the Good Shepherd, is responsible for your care. Thank Him that He is good. Thank Him that He is worthy of the responsibility of your care. Thank Him that you can trust Him to care for you. Thank Him that you are not your own shepherd. Thank Him that He does not leave you to wonder around and be destroyed. It is said that when a lamb continues to wander from the fold, a good shepherd will break the lamb's leg and place the crippled lamb on His shoulders so that the lamb will become accustomed to the closeness of His body, the lamb will feel His heartbeat, and become so familiar with His voice that the lamb will not stray again.

- Thank Him that he is willing to go after you when you stray from His care. Thank Him that He is willing to keep you close to His side when you are hurt and crippled. Thank Him that he is willing to do whatever is necessary to keep you from being devoured by the enemy.

God: The Object of Our Prayers

Jehovah-shammah: The Lord Is Present

Ezekiel 48:35 (NKJV)

The perimeter of the city will be six miles, and the name of the city from that day on will be: THE LORD IS THERE.

A new city and temple had been built for the presence of God. This would be the place where Jehovah would be, thus Jehovah-shammah, the Lord is there. Jehovah promised His presence among His people from the beginning. The presence of God gave victory in battle, direction to nations, and so on. Today we know the presence of God is no longer in a building. The presence of God is within us, the people of God. We are now living temples. According to 1 Corinthians 3:16, "Know ye not that ye are a temple of God, and that the Spirit of God dwells in you?"

Please read 1 Corinthians 3:16–17, 1 Corinthians 6:19, 2 Corinthians 6:16, and Ephesians 2:21.

God has made sure His presence is with His people. After the person of Jesus Christ ascended, the Holy Spirit was sent. Jesus said in John 14:16–18 that He would not leave us as orphans. He would send another comforter to abide with us forever. Hebrews 13:5 says that He will never leave nor forsake us. Psalm 139 asks where we could go from His presence. Maybe it would be helpful for you to read Psalms 139:7–12. From reading these verses, it sounds like we, His people, are stuck to God like glue. You cannot get away from His presence; hopefully you do not want to.

It is an awesome thing to think the presence of the Holy God lives within me. When I think about some of my actions, attitudes, and words, I cringe at the thought of exposing Holy God to my life. Oh, but I am so thankful that He will never leave me nor forsake me.

Remember, whatever frame of mind you are in, whatever place you go to, whatever behavior you are participating in, He is there.

I just want you to remember that wherever you go, Jehovah-shammah is present. When you feel so low that you do not think you can live, Jehovah-shammah is there also. When you present yourself for worship, He is there. Maybe it would be helpful if we remembered when we go to a cold, dry church service, Jehovah-shammah is there within us. He may be grieved because of the atmosphere, but you cannot say that He was not there.

As you pray today, get before the Lord in reverence, quiet yourself, and tell Him you acknowledge Him as Jehovah-shammah, the God who is there.

- Ask God to reveal any times you have grieved Him by places you have taken Him or behavior that has broken His heart. Ask God to make you aware of His presence in those times.

- Thank God that you cannot run or hide from His presence. Thank God that He lives within you, that you are the temple of the living God. Ask Him to cleanse your temple. Pray that you would make for Him a more acceptable abode.

- Thank Him that He is there in your troubles, in your fears, and in your pain.

- Thank Him that He is there to give you joy. Ask Him to fill you with joy.

He is there in good times, and He is there in bad times. He is there when you worship. I have often wondered what it must be like for those people who live without the presence of God in their lives. What would there be to live for? What could your spouse offer you in times of trouble if he or she had nothing of the Spirit of God within? What could I offer someone else without drawing from the presence of God living within me? Oh, thanks be unto the Living God that I will never have to know the answers to these questions.

CHAPTER 2

Relationship: The Connection of Our Prayers

How are we able to reach God with our prayers? How can I, a mortal person, reach the throne of the Holy God? "⁶But you, when you pray, go into your room, and when you have shut your door, pray to your Father who *is* in the secret *place;* and your Father who sees in secret will reward you openly. ⁸Therefore do not be like them. For your Father knows the things you have need of before you ask Him. ⁹In this manner, therefore, pray: Our Father in heaven, Hallowed be Your name" (Matthew 6:6, 8, 9). Pay attention to the references to your "Father." How are we able to reach God with our prayers? This Scripture tells us plainly. The key to God hearing your prayers is a relationship. We must have a relationship with God our Father.

In order for our prayers to be effective, there must be a relationship present, a father–child relationship. Let me assure you, if you do not have a relationship with the Father, you can say words all day long, but if there is no connection made between you and God, there is no joy in praying. Joy comes through the interaction between you and God. When you have intimacy with God, you cannot help but have joy.

If you are saved, your relationship with God began at the moment of your salvation. God lives within your heart, and when you become a Christian, the relationship you have with God is a permanent one.

"16For God so loved the world that He gave His only begotten Son, that whosoever believeth in Him should not perish but have everlasting life" (John 3:16). This verse teaches us that it is a relationship that is eternal and one that can never be lost.

John 9:31 (HCSB)

31Now we know that God does not hear sinners, but if anyone is a worshiper of God and does His will, He hears him.

Jesus healed sinners as a sign of His Lordship and His will. It was not based on the relationship that they had with Him. Most became believers. To be a sinner means to miss the mark, someone who has deviated from what God originally designed. To be a sinner is to miss the mark of what God created you to be. He created man originally to be pure and in perfect harmony with their creator. Because of Adam, you and I are not able to imagine that state. But as one fallen human being to another, have you come short of what God intended for you? Have you at all times and in all ways lived up to your God-given potential? If not, then you, my friend, have missed the mark. We have all missed the mark. We are all sinners. We are all lost without the cleansing blood of Jesus Christ. Thank God, we have a Savior.

This verse teaches us that a lost person can pray, but it is ineffective. A lost person's prayers will not move the hand of God. The only prayer He will hear from a lost person is a prayer asking for salvation. And when I say "hear," I mean that God would literally hear and be moved to action on behalf of the person. And that prayer, my dear friend, will move God's heart as well as His hand. God hears and moves on behalf of a person who is God fearing and saved through the blood of Jesus Christ. We read in 2 Chronicles 16:9, the eyes of the Lord run to and fro throughout the whole earth to show Himself strong on behalf of those whose heart is loyal to Him. After reading that verse, I picture the Lord leaning, looking intently, and searching for the person and situation where He can move. What a picture of a loving Lord.

When we are reverent and have an attitude of worship, then we are on our way to becoming a worshipper of God. The truth is we seek to know God, because it gives us pleasure. May I suggest it also gives God pleasure? The Scripture teaches that God loves and hears those who do His will. By doing His will, we please God and give Him joy. I do not know about you, but to think that I give God pleasure and joy and that I, little ole me, can please Him is pretty spectacular. I like to think of giving God pleasure in terms like "making His heart smile." If we would only seek His will instead of our own and be obedient, it would, quite frankly, take our breath away and astound us at what God is capable of doing in and through us. He has no limits! Why do we keep trying to place limits on Him?

James 5:16 (NKJV)

[16]Confess *your* trespasses to one another, and pray for one another, that ye may be healed. The effective, fervent prayer of a righteous man avails much.

The latter part of this verse tells us that our prayer lives are to be active. When we pray, we are making known our particular needs to God. Yes, He already knows what they are, but He *wants* us to have a relationship with Him. He desires for us to be close to Him. He wants us to tell Him our needs, but He also wants us to listen to His response.

A righteous man is someone who has conditioned his life by the standards of God, not his own. A righteous man is someone who, as a result of his relationship with God, walks with God. God wants us to abide by His rules and standards, because of the relationship that we have with the Father. It is a love relationship. The relationship and righteousness is not about Him demanding that we do so; it is about aligning ourselves to His standards, because we love Him and trust that what He says is best; it is about wanting to be where He is and wanting to please Him.

After the relationship is established, our prayer effectiveness as well as our joy is determined by the degree of intimacy in our relationship with God. "[8]Draw near to God and He will draw near to you. Cleanse *your* hands, sinners, and purify *your* hearts, double-minded people" (James 4:8) (HCSB). The phrase "draw near," in this instance, means to have communion with God in prayer as well as a desire to have fellowship with Him. In order to develop intimacy in our relationship we are required to draw near to Him through prayer. We must spend time with God and share our thoughts and feelings with Him. We have to become transparent before Him. We cannot try to hide things from God. We know that God knows all things, but somehow, we think if we just avoid talking to Him about certain things, He will eventually forget it—much like we operate in our human relationships.

Since the day Adam and Eve sinned, our natural tendency is to hide sin from God—just as they did in the garden. It is also our tendency to hide our true selves from those around us—just as Adam and Eve hid their nakedness from each other and from God. We try to hide our vulnerabilities from God and others; we do not want to be spiritually or emotionally naked before God or others. But in order to have true intimacy with God, we must allow ourselves to become transparent in His presence. As we do, we learn to trust that He will not hurt or reject us but that he loves us. As we learn to trust Him, we become comfortable in His presence. God's desire is to be with us and have intimacy with us. We must also desire to be with Him, to develop intimacy in our relationship with Him. I promise that you will never be disappointed, hurt, or rejected through intimacy with the One who loves you more than you can imagine.

When we have an intimacy with God, we will have a reverence toward God. We find our pleasure in being with Him, and we will have a deep desire within us to please Him. Having intimacy in our relationship with God develops:

- An emotional bond between you and God

- Loyalty between you and God

- Vulnerability between you and God

- An ability to know what hurts God and makes God happy

- Freedom to be ourselves when with Him

- Trust in the only One truly trustworthy

Joy in prayer, as well as effectiveness in prayer, is first related to our being a believer in Christ. To experience deep joy we must become a worshipper of God. Sometime we don't "feel" like worshipping God, and it is at those times we worship as an act of our will based on our desire to give Him pleasure as well as the pleasure and joy we have when we are in His presence.

Our joy and our effectiveness in prayer are related to our righteousness. What degree do we condition our lives to God's standards and His rules rather than our own? The more we conform to or mesh our lives with God, the more effective our prayer life becomes. The more intimacy we have with the God, the more joy we experience not only in prayer but in everything we do.

Nothing limits our relationship with God more than our own unwillingness to draw near to Him. "⁶Now without faith *it is* impossible to please *God,* for the one who draws near to must believe that He exists, and rewards those who seek Him" (Hebrews 11:6) (HCSB). We can draw near to God through prayer, through our sacrifice, and in our worship. We must believe that God is able and willing to answer our prayers. This is a person whom God hears when they pray.

Look at the above verse. If we want to please God, we must first believe that He is everything the Word of God declares Him to be. If we are to please God, we must also believe that He will reward us if we diligently seek Him. When we seek Him with our whole heart, knowing Him is our greatest reward.

RELATIONSHIP: THE CONNECTION OF OUR PRAYERS

Devotionals

God: The Connection of Our Prayers

Salvation by Grace Through Faith in Christ

Ephesians 2:1–8 (NKJV)

¹And you *He made alive,* who were dead in trespasses and sins, ²in which you once walked according to the course of this world, according to the prince of the air, the spirit who now works in the sons of disobedience, ³among whom also we all once conducted ourselves in the lusts of our flesh, fulfilling the desires of the flesh and of the mind, and were by nature children of wrath, just as the others. ⁴But God, who is rich in mercy, because of His great love with which He loved us, ⁵even when we were dead in trespasses, made us alive together with Christ (by grace you have been saved), ⁶and raised *us* up together, and made *us* sit together in the heavenly *places* in Christ Jesus, ⁷that in the ages to come He might show the exceeding riches of His grace in His kindness toward us in Christ Jesus. ⁸For by grace you have been saved through faith, and that not of yourselves; *it is* the gift of God.

In this passage from Ephesians, there are several references to unbelievers being "dead" in their trespasses and sins. It gives us a picture of how we who were "dead" were made alive in Christ. We have been raised from death to life in Christ! Praise His name!! What about the unbelievers who are still spiritually dead? Remember, God only hears unbelievers' prayers as they acknowledge Him and repent. Who is praying for them?

Have you ever stopped to think about who prayed that the Lord would draw you to Himself in conviction? Was it a parent, a Sunday school teacher, someone from another church, or a neighbor? Maybe you do not know who that person was, but aren't you thankful that they prayed for you?

During your prayer time today, stop and think about the person(s) who held you up before God while you were unable to pray for yourself. You were spiritually "dead"; a dead person can do nothing for himself. If that person is still alive, you might want to call or write a letter to thank the person for the concern for your soul. Thank him or her for taking the time to pray for you. Let the individual know the prayers are appreciated. We all need to be reminded of the importance of praying for unbelievers.

Unbelievers are helpless concerning their own salvation. They cannot be saved without the drawing of the Holy Spirit into their lives. And they cannot force the Holy Spirit to draw them. They are dependent on God to do the drawing. Just as I stated earlier concerning not being able to make my heart beat or make myself take the next breath, I could not make myself feel the conviction of the Lord. It would never dawn on me to feel bad about my own sin if it were not for the Spirit of God.

Sinners are totally dependent on someone else to pray for God to draw them to Himself in conviction. Perhaps God automatically convicts and draws everyone without anyone ever praying for them, but I would rather be like the friend Jesus described in Luke 11:5 and the following verses. This person was persistent in his asking, and he got results. Jesus then taught that we are to keep asking, seeking, and knocking. Jesus continued by saying that we being evil know how to give good gifts, but how much more the Father would give the Holy Spirit to those who ask. I think it might be beneficial to ask for the salvation of the souls of your loved ones.

Why do we not see more people saved in our local churches? Have we failed to lift them up before the throne of God? Have we stopped praying for conviction to fall on our family, friends, and neighbors? Why does Satan distract us from praying for the lost? Maybe he believes that by preventing us from praying for the lost, he will be able to take many of them to hell with him.

Do not forget, hell is very real. I believe that if we truly believed in the reality of hell, we would pray more earnestly for those we love to be saved. Let us begin again to pray for our lost family members to be saved. Pray for unborn children. Pray that children will be saved at an early age. Pray for their hearts to be softened. Pray for God's hand to be upon children's lives, that they would grow up with a devotion to Almighty God. Pray that your children believe the Word of God wholeheartedly and see the futility of the world's ways. Pray for your friends, family, neighbors, and so on. Let us pray for those who are unable to pray for themselves. For we, too, were once unable to pray for ourselves.

Today as you pray, remember to enter His gates with thanksgiving and His courts with praise. Sing a song to Him if you would like to. Some points to use as you pray:

- Thank God for the relationship you have with Him through salvation.

- Thank God for the ones who prayed for you when you were "dead" in trespasses and sin.

- Pray a blessing for the people who prayed for you.

- Pray for the lost to be saved. Mention them specifically by name.

- Pray for the unborn and the little children to know Him.

- Pray for increased devotion to Him.

- Thank Him for the privilege of His presence.

Relationship: The Connection of Our Prayers

Our Relationship with the Father

In the last devotional, we thanked God for salvation and those who prayed for us. In this devotional, I want to spend more time thinking about what our relationship with the Father really means.

Ephesians 2:1–8 (NKJV)

¹And you *He made alive,* who were dead in trespasses and sins, ²in which you once walked according to the course of this world, according to the prince of the air, the spirit who now works in the sons of disobedience, ³among whom also we all once conducted ourselves in the lusts of our flesh, fulfilling the desires of the flesh and of the mind, and were by nature children of wrath, just as the others. ⁴But God, who is rich in mercy, because of His great love with which He loved us, ⁵even when we were dead in trespasses, made us alive together with Christ (by grace you have been saved), ⁶and raised *us* up together, and made *us* sit together in the heavenly *places* in Christ Jesus, ⁷that in the ages to come He might show the exceeding riches of His grace in His kindness toward us in Christ Jesus. ⁸For by grace you have been saved through faith, and that not of yourselves; *it is* the gift of God.

Think about each part of Ephesians 2:1–8, about what it means to you. For example, verse 1 says that there is a part of you that is alive that was once dead. You once were caught in sin. Verse 2 says because of that sin, you walked according to the course of this world. Praise God that you are free from the snare of sin, you are free from this world's ways, and you are free from the prince of the power of the air. Praise Him! Continue to thank God for what this Scripture says about you.

John 3:16 (NKJV)

[16]For God so loved the world that He gave His only begotten Son, that whoever believes in him should not perish but have everlasting life.

John 17:3 (NKJV)

[3]And this is eternal life, that they may know You, the only true God, and Jesus Christ whom You have sent.

Romans 8:35–39 (NKJV)

[35]Who shall separate us from the love of Christ? *Shall* tribulation, or distress, or persecution, or famine, or nakedness, or peril, or sword? [36]As it is written: *"For Your sake we are killed all day long; we are accounted as sheep for the slaughter."* [37]Yet in all these things we are more than conquerors through Him who loved us. [38]For I am persuaded that neither death nor life, nor angels nor principalities nor powers, nor things present nor things to come, [39]nor height nor depth, nor any other created thing, shall be able to separate us from the love of God which is in Christ Jesus our Lord.

John 17:20–26 (NKJV)

[20]"I do not pray for these alone, but also for those who will believe in Me through their word; [21]that they all my be one, as You, Father, *are* in Me, and I in You; that they also may be one in Us, that the world may believe that You sent Me. [22]And the glory which You gave Me I have given them, that they may be one just as We are one: [23]I in them, and You in Me; that they may be made perfect in one, and that the world may know that You have sent Me, and have loved them as You have loved Me. [24]Father, I desire that they also whom you gave Me may be with Me where I am, that they may behold My glory which You have given Me; for You loved Me before the foundation of the world. [25]O righteous Father! The world has not known You, but I have known You; and these have known that You sent Me. [26]And I have declared to them Your name,

and will declare *it*, that the love with which You loved Me may be in them, and I in them."

John 14:1–3 (NKJV)

¹**"Let not your heart be troubled; you believe in God, believe also in Me. ²In My Father's house are many mansions; if *it were* not *so,* I would have told you. I go to prepare a place for you. ³And if I go and prepare a place for you, I will come again and receive you to Myself; that where I am, *there* you may be also."**

As you pray today:

- Thank God that you will never perish. Do you realize what that means? It means you will never be separated from God!

- Thank Him that you know the only true God. By knowing Him, the source of life, you have eternal life. There is nothing that can separate us from the love of God. Romans 8:35–39 mentions many things that cannot separate you from Him. Read through each one, and thank Him that each thing mentioned cannot separate you from Him. We have been made more than conquerors through Him who loved us. He is the conqueror, and He gave us the victory! Hallelujah! Praise God!

Do you realize that Jesus prayed for you? We are those who would believe through the word that John 17:20 is talking about.

- Thank God that He prayed for you.

- Thank God that we are one with Him. God loves us as much as He loves Jesus—yes, that is what the Scripture says.

- Thank God we will one day be where He is, and we will behold His glory.

- Thank God for preparing a place suited just for you.

- Thank God that He will come again for you—that He will not leave you behind.

I now ask that you open your Bible and pray these Scriptures right back to God. It is His Word; it is powerful. He did, in fact, create the universe by speaking it into existence. Spend whatever time you need to pray these Scriptures carefully back to God in praise.

What does it mean that you have a relationship with the God of the universe? It means you are attached to the vine and that you have access to everything that belongs to the Father. It also means you are never alone; He will never leave you nor forsake you. It means He is your Provider and Deliverer, along with a host of other things. It means you are His child. Rejoice!

To end your prayer time today, read the above paragraph again. Read each sentence, and praise Him for the truth recorded there. Pray it back to Him with a grateful heart.

Relationship: The Connection of Our Prayers

Increasing My Devotion to Him

James 4:8 (NKJV)

[8]**Draw near to God and He will draw near to you. Cleanse** *your* **hand,** *you* **sinners; and purify** *your* **hearts,** *you* **double-minded.**

Psalms 73:28 (NKJV)

[28]**But** *it is* **good for me to draw near to God; I have put my trust in the Lord GOD, that I may declare all Your works.**

As you may remember, to draw near to God means to have communion with God in prayer and the desired and cherished fellowship with Him. I do not know exactly where you are in your walk with the Father, but I do know that no matter where you are, there is ground to be covered. You may have experienced deep intimacy with the Lord in the past. If you have, I am sure that you want that again and much more for the future. So, no matter where you are, it is my prayer that you will have a desire to go further still.

I want you to spend your time in prayer today, asking God to increase your devotion toward Him. Please pray each part specifically and separately. Pray it until you mean it.

Lord, please:

1. Increase my desire to spend time with You in prayer.

2. Increase my capacity to love You more.

3. Increase my understanding of who You are as my Father as well as Almighty God.

4. Increase the depth of my prayers. Help me to know how to pray and for whom. Help me get past surface things.

5. Increase my willingness to release and use any gifts the Holy Spirit has placed within me.

6. Increase my willingness to be obedient to Your Word.

7. Increase my willingness and ability to hear Your voice.

8. Increase my willingness to get up early and spend time with You.

9. Increase my boldness in witnessing for You.

10. Increase the intimacy between us. Help me to be willing to be transparent with You.

11. Increase my desire to seek You with my whole heart.

12. Increase my submission to Your will and Your Lordship.

13. Increase my joy in spending time in Your presence.

Please feel free to add any other desire from your heart to His. If you are sincere when you pray these things, get ready to be obedient, as He begins to move in your life.

Relationship: The Connection of Our Prayers

Coming Before His Presence

Today let's begin by reading some Scripture about His presence.

Psalms 16:11 (NKJV)

[11]You will show me the path of life; in Your presence *is* fullness of joy; at Your right hand *are* pleasures forevermore.

Psalms 31:19–20 (NKJV)

[19]Oh, how great *is* Your goodness, which You have laid up for those who fear You, *which* You have prepared for those who trust in You in the presence of the sons of men! [20]You shall hide them in the secret place of Your presence from the plots of man; You shall keep them secretly in a pavilion from the strife of tongues.

Psalms 139:7 (NKJV)

[7]Where can I go from Your Spirit? Or where can I flee from Your presence?

1 Chronicles 16:27 (NKJV)

[27]Honor and majesty *are* before Him; strength and gladness are in His place.

Psalms 140:13 (NKJV)

[13]Surely the righteous shall give thanks to Your name; the upright shall dwell in Your presence.

Psalms 95:1–7 (NKJV)

¹Oh come let us sing to the LORD! Let us shout joyfully to the Rock of our salvation. ²Let us come before His presence with thanksgiving; let us shout joyfully to Him with psalms. ³For the LORD *is* the great God, and the great King above all gods. ⁴In His hand *are* the deep places of the earth; the heights of the hills *are* His also. ⁵The sea *is* His, for He made it; and His hands formed the dry *land.* ⁶Oh come, let us worship and bow down; let us kneel before the LORD our Maker. ⁷For He *is* our God, and we *are* the people of His pasture, and the sheep of His hand.

Psalms 100:1–5 (NKJV)

¹Make a joyful shout to the LORD, all you lands! ²Serve the LORD with gladness; come before His presence with singing. ³Know that the LORD, He *is* God; it *is* He *who* has made us, and not we ourselves; we *are* His people and the sheep of His pasture. ⁴Enter into His gates with thanksgiving, *and* into His courts with praise. Be thankful to Him, *and* bless His name. ⁵For the LORD *is* good; His mercy *is* everlasting and His truth *endures* to all generations.

Let's think about the wonderful privilege of being able to come before His presence. Hopefully, by this time in our study, you are experiencing a deeper level of expectancy and joy of being in God's presence. If not, keep asking Him to take you deeper.

By reading the Scriptures for today, you will find some wonderful things about being in God's presence. There is joy in His presence. We have protection in His presence. His presence is everywhere. Glory and honor are in His presence. The righteous dwell in His presence. It is so awesome to be in His presence, and it is my earnest desire that you know the joy of being in His presence.

There are things we are to do when we come into His presence. We are to come before His presence with thanksgiving. We are to shout joyfully to Him with psalms. We are to serve the Lord with gladness. We are to come before His presence with singing. Please read Psalms 95:1–7 and Psalms 100:1–5 again. Try to glean all the nourishment that you can from these two passages. Pray or praise them back to the Father.

Before you begin praying, get a pen and some paper and carefully go through each Scripture and list each thing that you can thank God for. I will get you started.

Psalms 95:1–7

- Thank Him that you can come before His presence.

- Thank Him that he has given you a voice to sing to Him or to speak praises to Him.

- Thank Him that He is your Rock of Salvation, that He is solid and unmovable.

- Thank Him that He is the King above all gods.

- Thank Him that He is the Great God—the only God.

Continue until you feel like you have covered everything in these Scriptures. There are many more things to praise Him for within these passages.

There is a song I would like to leave you with today. After you have praised God for His presence, use this song to worship Him. If you know the song, sing it unto the Lord. If not, quote it to Him as you have the Scripture passages.

> In His presence there is joy beyond all measure,
> And at His feet peace of mind can still be found.
> If you have a need I know He has the answer.
> Reach out and claim it, for you are standing on Holy Ground.
> You are standing on Holy Ground,
> And I know that there are angels all around.
> Let us praise Jesus now.
> You are standing in His presence on Holy Ground.
> (Geron Davis 1960. Meadowgreen Group, 54 Music Sq. E., Suite 305, Nashville, TN 37203.)

Relationship: The Connection of Our Prayers

His Relationship Is Permanent

In this last devotional on our relationship with the Father, I would like you to think about the fact that nothing can change or take away that relationship. It is permanent. In this life, most of us have lost someone whom we love in death. When couples marry, they never really think about the fact that one of them will probably be left alone. It happens all the time: young men and women die and leave a spouse and small children behind. When a mother gives birth to her baby, her mind is not thinking of losing that child in death, but she is dwelling on all the wonderful days of joy ahead. But the sad fact is every day, many mothers around the world experience the horrible pain of losing a child to death.

Most, if not all, of us have lost someone precious through some unforeseen set of circumstances. In this life, it happens to someone somewhere every day. We have all thought, *I could not live without you*, only to have to learn how to walk around and try to function with a new awareness of a totally different kind of death. Divorce brings this kind of death, as does losing other deep relationships. Sometimes we have to grieve the loss of our health or the health of someone we love deeply. This kind of loss brings the death of a way of life. Life is full of losses.

I grew up in a very unstable environment, where alcoholism and abuse dictated everything that occurred in life. Due to these difficult conditions, I grew up with an incredible need to have someone love me completely. I used to say I wanted to know the security of that love so completely that I could relax and stop holding my breath. I was holding my breath in the sense of just waiting until the next moment, when I knew that whatever crumb of love I had been thrown would be gone. I wanted love so desperately that I would open my heart at the least indication of love, and time after time, I was hurt. It happened over and over, until I was so hardened by hurt that I built up walls so high and thick that most people would have been scared to approach me. All the while, I wanted more than anything to find the person who would love me enough to scale the walls.

I guess growing up feeling like you were not worthy of someone loving you makes you afraid to trust love. You get in the mind-set of thinking; *Nobody loved me before, so why would anyone love me now?* Even in my severe pain, I wanted desperately to find someone who would never leave me nor forsake me.

Sad as it may be, I was right. No person can say that they will love you forever. They cannot promise you that they will never leave you. They cannot promise that they will always love you. It only takes one heartbeat to change or cancel a promise someone makes about never leaving you. The truth is that special someone may be gone without you ever getting the chance to say good-bye.

One misunderstanding or mistake is all it takes for a relationship to die. You are no longer loved like you hoped that you would always be. I have spent a lot of time and energy searching for that security only to realize that if I ever felt like I had it, my trust would be in the wrong place.

God is the only One who can make those claims and keep those promises. He is the only One who can actually love us forever. He is the only One who loves you completely and unconditionally. He is the only One who will never leave you nor forsake you. "⁶So *we are* always confident, knowing that while we are at home in the body we are absent from the Lord. ⁷For we walk by faith, not by sight. ⁸We are confident, yes, well pleased rather to be absent from the body and to be present with the Lord" (2 Corinthians 5:6–8) (NKJV). To be absent from the body is to be present with the Lord. When He says He will never leave us, He is serious.

In John 17, Jesus prayed that the Father and Son would be one with us, so we are. Regardless of whether we feel it, He gave us the Holy Spirit to indwell us forever. "¹⁶And I will pray the Father, and He will give you another Helper, that He may abide with you forever" (John 14:16) (NKJV). He is always with us, always present. What He is saying is that when we accept Jesus, He makes His abode in us through the Holy Spirit. Even death cannot separate us from Him. To die is to be present with the Lord.

As you enter His presence today, do so with reverence and humility. Enter with thanksgiving in your heart and a song of praise on your lips.

- Spend time today thanking God that His relationship is permanent.

- Thank Him that His relationship can be trusted.

- Thank Him that He does love you completely.

- Thank Him that nothing we can do will ever make His love change.

- Thank Him that we are safe in His arms.

- Read Ephesians 1:13 and 4:30 in your Bible.

- Thank Him that you have been sealed by the Holy Spirit until the day of redemption; thank Him that nothing can change that, praise God!

CHAPTER 3

Humility: The Position of Our Prayers

2 Chronicles 7:14 (NKJV)

[14]If My people who are called by My name will humble themselves, and pray and seek My face, and turn from their wicked ways, then I will hear from heaven, and will forgive their sin and heal their land.

1 Kings 8:54 (NKJV)

[54]And so it was, when Solomon had finished praying all this prayer and supplication to the LORD, that he arose from before the altar of the LORD, from kneeling on his knees with his hands spread up to heaven.

Matthew 26:39 (NKJV)

[39]He went a little farther and fell on His face, and prayed, saying, "O My Father, if it is possible, let this cup pass from Me; nevertheless, not as I will, but as You *will*."

Matthew 18:4 (NKJV)

[4]Therefore whoever humbles himself as this little child is the greatest in the kingdom of heaven.

Romans 14:11 (NKJV)

¹¹**For it is written:** *"As I live, says the LORD, every knee shall bow to Me, and every tongue shall confess to God."*

Philippians 2:10-11 (NKJV)

¹⁰**That at the name of Jesus every knee should bow, of those in heaven, and of those on earth, and of those under the earth,** ¹¹**and** *that* **every tongue should confess that Jesus Christ** *is* **Lord, to the glory of God the Father.**

James 4:6 (NKJV)

⁶**But He gives more grace. Therefore He says:** *"God resists the proud, but gives grace to the humble."*

To be effective in prayer, we must have humility. Over and over in Scripture, we are instructed to humble ourselves before God. In the above Scriptures, humility is contrasted with pride. When we think of a proud person, we think of one who tries to elevate himself; one who thinks himself better than others; he might be arrogant. The word "proud" is sometimes associated with the rejection of God. So then, humility describes one who is lowly in attitude or position. To be humble is to recognize our true condition, which is totally dependent on God. Without God, we are nothing and can do nothing. Therefore, the ground is level at the foot of the cross; no one is elevated above anyone else. We must all come to Jesus the same way, offering nothing except ourselves.

Humility is a choice. We see in the above verses that Solomon bowed before the Lord and that Jesus Himself bowed in prayer. As the verses from Romans and Philippians tell us, every knee will bow before Him. To be humble means to yield everything to God. We are acknowledging His importance. By bowing before Him, we are exalting Him. Humility is an attitude, a motive of the heart.

Jesus was a prime example of humility. He <u>never</u> made Himself a superior person; He sacrificed Himself. If the Son of God was humble and prayed with humility, how then can we possibly think that we should pray any other way?

How many times during the past week have you bowed on your knees before God? How many times in the last month? Have you ever bowed on your knees before God? How do you imagine that you will respond to the Lord when you first see Him in heaven? I am willing to say that most of us, if not all, will bow down before Him, probably as low to the ground as we can get. I want to ask you to think about something. Will God be any different then than He is now? No, He will not. The difference will be in us. Rather than praying to God, whom we have never seen, we will be standing before Him face to face! Don't you think that God deserves to have us bow before Him now also? I do. After all, we are praying to the King of Kings and Lord of Lords.

Do you have to be on your knees for God to hear your prayers? No, you do not, but I believe that it sure removes any doubt of who is in charge. We certainly aren't in charge, even though we sometimes think we are. God is the commander, and He is solely in charge. Bowing before God in prayer does the following:

- Positions you in submission to the One you are praying to.

- Positions you as vulnerable to the Master.

- Reminds you who is Lord.

- Is an expression of devotion that you feel for your Father.

- Is a position of worship.

- Is a position of purpose. There is no doubt of our purpose; we are less likely to be disturbed or distracted.

- Expresses an attitude of reverence.

Matthew 18:1–5 (NKJV)

¹**At that time the disciples came to Jesus, saying, "Who then is greatest in the kingdom of heaven?" ²Then Jesus called a little child to Him, set him in the midst of them, ³and said, "Assuredly, I say to you, unless you are converted and become as little children, you will by no means enter the kingdom of heaven. ⁴Therefore whoever humbles himself as this little child is the greatest in the**

kingdom of heaven. ⁵Whoever receives one little child like this in My name receives Me.

Mark 10:15 (NKJV)

¹⁵Assuredly, I say to you, whoever does not receive the kingdom of God as a child will by no means enter it."

Children are good examples of humility. Jesus taught us that we are to become like little children. Children trust, they are open and honest, they are happy to be with the one they love, they are loyal, they are expressive, they are teachable, and they are joyful and happy. What an impressive list to try to live up to. Are we as little children before our God?

Children depend on their parents for the following:

- Nourishment

- Cleaning up their messes

- Protection

- Clothing

- Love

- To teach them about life

- To teach them how to avoid danger

- Mercy

- Training to hear and obey their parent's voice

- Training to become good parents themselves

- Training in interpersonal relationships

Will you take the above list and ask yourself if you rely on God in these ways? We should depend on God for all of the above. If we depend on another source for these needs, you will inevitably wind up with inaccurate, incomplete, and destructive information.

Today we seem to be afraid of what other people will think if we get on our knees in public. The church should be a place to bow before God freely, to worship Him. I have heard many people say there have been times when they wanted to bow before God at the altar but were afraid of being perceived as abnormal or sinful. They worried about what someone else would think of them. If we want to be free to worship, we must break away from that way of thinking. We must realize that God is God, and we must please Him before anyone else.

I was saved in and taught in a church where it would have been abnormal to pray standing or sitting rather than on your knees. At times, we gathered at the altar, all got on our knees, and in unity cried out to Holy God. I am so thankful to have had that model for prayer. As a child, I was often asked to lead in prayer within the church service. I always got on my knees to pray, as I had been taught, and I believe my prayer life is richer for having been introduced to praying in that fashion. I wonder how we have come so far from our forefather's pattern of prayer.

I personally believe Satan has inched his way into our lives regarding prayer, because he knows the power of prayer. I have watched an entire generation miss out on the joys of kneeling before God, because my generation believed the lies of the Devil that questioned the benefit of kneeling before God to pray. Yes, God can hear you in any position, but if it isn't important to kneel before the Lord, why is every knee going to bow and every tongue confess that Jesus is Lord? I encourage you to make it a practice of bowing on your knees before God in prayer. Try it for one month and see if you notice a difference in your prayer time.

Humility is more than simply getting on your knees. It is an attitude of the heart. It's an attitude that has a correct estimation of who we are and who God is. Humility also means piety toward God. Piety means loyalty to God and devotion to godly and religious duties. Are you devoted to God and His ways? To have joy in praying and have an effective prayer life, we are to be humble before our God.

HUMILITY: THE POSITION OF OUR PRAYERS

Devotionals

Humility: The Position of Our Prayers

Beautify the Living Temple

2 Chronicles 7:14 (NKJV)
14If My people who are called by My name will humble themselves, and pray and seek My face, and turn from their wicked ways, then I will hear from heaven, and will forgive their sin and heal their land.

Several years ago, my pastor, said he believed this verse described where we are as a church. We had built a new addition onto our building to increase our Sunday school space. We paid the debt and dedicated the building as a place of worship. As a church, we had beautified His house. Now it was time for us, His people, to deal with our own hearts. I realize that you are not part of my local church, but you are an important part of the body of Christ, whether here or somewhere else.

The focus I believe now needs to be on our own hearts and lives. We need to beautify the living temples of the Almighty God. We are His temple. If you are a born-again believer, the Holy Spirit of God lives within you. What kind of junk needs to be cleaned out of our hearts and our lives? Are there some areas where the Lord is not welcome to do business in your life? Are there things you would not be willing to expose to the cleansing light of the Holy Spirit and the Word of God? Is there anything you would withhold from His hand? These are powerful questions to consider.

Notice that the Scripture from 2 Chronicles says we must be His people, called by His name. I am assuming that you have already dealt with this issue. If not, do not wait another minute: do it now! The next thing that this verse teaches is that the people are to humble themselves. I take that to mean as a matter of our own will. It is something that we must choose to do; God will not force us to do so. We must choose to humble ourselves before God.

Remember that to humble means to recognize our condition as totally dependent on God, to recognize and acknowledge Him for whom He is. During your prayer time today, I encourage you to:

- Make sure that your salvation is real.

- Thank Him that you are one of His, called by His name.

- Make a choice to humble yourself before the Lord of heaven.

- Pray for the cleansing of your heart.

- Seek His face, that is, to seek intimacy with Him.

- Ask Him if there is any wicked way within you that He wants to point out.

- Ask Him if there is something or somebody that you need to turn away from.

- Thank Him that He has heard your prayer.

- Thank Him that His promise is to heal your land—that is, your heart, your life, your family, your finances—whatever needs His healing touch.

After you have finished praying this personal prayer, please pray these same things for your local church body as a whole. Pray that each part of His body will seek His face in intimacy. Pray that as a body of believers your church will be able to be humble before Him, and as they are in His presence, that He will point out to each person individually what He wants to cleanse within them. Pray for your church leadership. Then pray for the entire body of Christ to be cleansed by the washing of the water of the Word.

Humility: The Position of Our Prayers

Pride Is Dangerous

James 4:6 (NKJV)

⁶**But He gives more grace. Therefore He says: "*God resists the proud, but gives grace to the humble.*"**

Proverbs 16:18 (NKJV)

¹⁸**Pride *goes* before destruction and a haughty spirit before a fall.**

Proverbs 13:10 (NKJV)

¹⁰**By pride comes nothing but strife, but with the well-advised *is* wisdom.**

1 John 2:16 (NKJV)

¹⁶**For all that is in the world—the lust of the flesh, the lust of the eyes, and the pride of life—are not of the Father but are of the world.**

Pride can be a very subtle thing. Sometimes I can see pride in the way a person walks or stands. You often hear pride dripping from lips, as people give testimony in church. You don't have to listen to a person but about thirty seconds to hear pride pushing itself to the surface of the conversation. The funny thing is, when we are in the middle of pride, it is very hard to see it within ourselves. It is one of those things that sneak up on us. We all want and need to feel loved and appreciated, and we feel obligated to tell someone that they did a good job. Our efforts to encourage others can sometimes be used by the enemy to cause pride in another. No, we should not stop encouraging others, but we need to keep the pride patrol active and on duty in our own lives.

Pride is very dangerous to our Christian walk, because the verse from James says God resists the proud. The word "resist" means God sets Himself in opposition to or in array against, or to set an army against. That is pretty strong language. The good news is that if we can recognize the pride in our own lives and humble ourselves before God, we have a promise of more grace. What more could we want than a promise of more of His empowering presence?

Just as a reminder: are you preparing yourself for prayer? Are you remembering to come before His presence with thanksgiving in your heart? Are you coming in reverence, acknowledging His Lordship over you? Quiet yourself and ask that the Holy Spirit help you pray.

After you have read the Scriptures listed, ask God to deal with the pride in your life. Ask Him to point out any area of pride to you. Take each Scripture and ask Him to show you if that aspect of pride is a problem in your life. For example, in Proverb 13, pride causes contention. Are there times when your pride gets in the way of losing an argument? I have seen people fight something to the end, all the while knowing they were wrong. I believe we could safely say that is a pride issue. Do you want things, because you feel embarrassed if you don't have everything your neighbor has? If so, it is probably a pride issue. There may be others that the Lord wants to point out to you: listen and respond.

I find that it is a good idea to get out a notebook and record anything that He brings to your mind related to pride and yourself. After you have listed and talked to God about each thing, you may need to repent and receive His cleansing flow. It feels so good to stand under His healing stream.

Humility: The Position of Our Prayers

Humbling Ourselves in Prayer

Romans 8:26–27 (NKJV)
²⁶Likewise the Spirit also helps in our weaknesses. For we do no know what we should pray for as we ought, but the Spirit Himself makes intercession for us with groanings which cannot be uttered. ²⁷Now He who searches the hearts knows what the mind of the Spirit *is*, because He makes intercession for the saints according to *the will of God*.

A part of humility is recognizing that we are completely dependent on God. This is true for when we pray as well. Yes, we must make a commitment to pray consistently whether we "feel" like it or not. It would be very misleading to say that we will always feel the urging of the Holy Spirit to pray. When you do feel that urging, it is very important that you stop what you are doing and pray. God does not urge you to do anything unless it is of great necessity that it be done. You may never know what God did through your act of obedience, but trust Him anyway.

Romans 8:26 says that the Holy Spirit helps us in our weaknesses. When we do not know what to pray, the Spirit makes intercession for us. How amazing! Have you ever been at a place in your prayer where the words were just not there? Your words just could not express the depth of what you felt. That is when the Holy Spirit wants to pray through you. As both verses say, we really don't know what we should pray, or how we should pray. Without the Holy Spirit's direction, we are clueless as to what God's will might be in any given situation. The Holy Spirit and the Father work together in perfect harmony. The Holy Spirit only prays the will of God the Father.

I encourage you to ask the Holy Spirit to pray through you. Ask Him to show you how to pray and for whom. In praying this way, we acknowledge our dependence on God, even in praying. We cannot do it alone. We can say words, but to pray the will of God takes the Holy Spirit's intercession.

Often, in my own life, I will begin to feel restless in my spirit. There is a feeling I simply cannot explain. It comes from the depth of my being. I have learned over the years that I need to get alone and pray. It is usually the Holy Spirit wanting to reveal something to me through prayer.

Humbling ourselves before God in prayer is recognizing our dependence on Him (the Holy Spirit) to be able to pray effectively. It is acknowledging our lack of knowledge and ability to pray in God's will. It is asking the Holy Spirit to pray through us. Humbling ourselves before God in prayer is also recognizing his leadership in our spirit for times of special prayer.

Prepare yourself for prayer through the things you have already learned. Kneel before Him in reverence and awe today. Submit yourself to His authority. Begin by thanking and praising Him for His goodness and mercy, for His power that works in your life. Just praise Him. He is worthy of praise.

As you have your prayer time today:

- Ask God to release within you the gifts of the Holy Spirit that will enable you to pray in God's will.

- Ask God to begin to teach you to allow the Holy Spirit to pray through you. After you ask these things, then you must trust what He says in Romans. May you have a blessed time with the Lord today!

- Ask God to teach you a new and deeper way to praise Him. Some time ago, I told God I felt like I always said the same things when praising Him. I asked Him to give me new things to say, and for almost an hour, I praised Him for things I had not thought of before. He is faithful.

Humility: The Position of Our Prayers

Low Self-Esteem

Psalm 10:4 (NKJV)
⁴**The wicked in his proud countenance does not seek God; God is in none of his thoughts.**

When we think of pride, we think of someone feeling or thinking more highly of themselves than they should. And truly, that is a prideful attitude. There is also another attitude that is just as much prideful in nature. That is an attitude of low self-esteem. It is still all about *me*. Let me see if I can draw it for you.

I'm awful!!!!   ↔   **"Me"**   ↔   **I'm good!!!!**

The focus is always on me in either situation. When people have low self-esteem, their need is to be built up. They feel it necessary to let others know they are really pretty worthless. Of course, there are degrees of this attitude just as there are degrees to the traditional puffed-up attitude of pride. Those with low self-esteem are hoping once others know how worthless they feel, something will be said or done to convince them otherwise. If someone says something positive, it is supposed to lift them up, if only for a moment.

Those with puffed-up pride tend to lift themselves up, while the other folks hope against hope that someone else will make them feel better. A puffed-up person needs to feel good about self, a person with low self-esteem needs to feel good about self, see the similarities? One is hoping someone else will build him up; the other takes the shortcut and jumps right in and builds himself up.

This kind of need can be dangerous to a Christian. If much of our energy is focused on feeling good about ourselves, when do we have time to hear God? I believe that whether the thoughts of self are too high or too low, our focus is on us rather than on God and His work.

Be careful when thoughts of self and self-protection occupy a greater part of your thought life than God. Ask yourself, "Do I spend more energy and thoughts on increasing myself or increasing God?" "[30]He must increase, but I *must* decrease" (John 3:30) (NKJV). By implementing this verse, many of our struggles would cease. We would be focused on God, not on ourselves.

After you have prepared yourself for prayer:

- Ask God to show you if you have an issue with needing to be lifted up by those around you. Do you need others to tell you what a good job you have done? Do you find yourself feeling bad toward yourself and needing others to prove you wrong? Ask God to reveal any sense of low self-esteem within you.

- Ask God to give you security and esteem only in Him.

- Pray that God will help you esteem Him higher than you do self.

Remember, humility is the *correct* estimation of who you are and who God is. Humility is not constantly putting yourself down or doing without material things. To have a correct estimation is your goal; it does not need to be too high nor too low. My dear friend, you are of great value, but only through the blood of Jesus.

- Praise Him for the value He places on you.

- Ask God to help you see yourself through His eyes.

Humility: The Position of Our Prayers

God Knows the Secrets of Your Heart

Matthew 23:12 (NKJV)

¹²And whoever exalts himself will be humbled, and he who humbles himself will be exalted.

Isaiah 14:13–15 (NKJV)

¹³For you have said in your heart: "I will ascend into heaven, I will exalt my throne above the stars of God; I will also sit on the mount of the congregation on the farthest sides of the north; ¹⁴I will ascend above the heights of the clouds, I will be like the Most High." ¹⁵Yet you shall be brought down to Sheol, to the lowest depths of the Pit.

Proverbs 16:5 (NKJV)

⁵Everyone proud in heart *is* an abomination to the LORD; *though they join* forces none will go unpunished.

Psalms 44:21 (NKJV)

²¹Would not God search this out? For He knows the secrets of the heart.

Hebrews 4:12 (NKJV)

¹²For the word of God *is* living and powerful, and sharper than any two-edged sword, piercing even to the division of soul and spirit, and of joints and marrow, and is a discerner of the thoughts and intents of the heart.

Matthew 15:18–19 (NKJV)

¹⁸But those things which proceed out of the mouth come from the heart and they defile a man. ¹⁹For out of the heart

proceed evil thoughts, murders, adulteries, fornications, thefts, false witness, blasphemies.

In Isaiah 14, we see that wanting to exalt himself got Satan into trouble. Notice the part that says, "You have said in your heart: I will." The heart is the seat of pride as well as the seat of all other emotions and motives. God knows the desires of your heart.

We see in the above Scripture that the Word of God is a discerner of the thoughts and intents of the heart. We also see that what proceeds out of the mouth comes from the heart, and the things of the heart precede evil; that is what defiles a man. Whatever is in our hearts comes out in our thoughts, words, and actions. "[45]A good man out of the good treasure of his heart brings forth good; and an evil man out of the evil treasure of his heart brings forth evil. For out of the abundance of the heart his mouth speaks" (Luke 6:45) (NKJV).

Pride was found in Satan's heart. He decided that he wanted to exalt himself and be like the Most High God. Sad to say, but we as the church of the Most High God have exalted Satan too much also. If you continue reading in the book of Isaiah, you will see that when we finally see Satan for who he is, we will be amazed and say, "Is this the man who made the earth tremble, who shook kingdoms?" (Isaiah 14:16) (NKJV)

I wonder if we talk about Satan too much, if we give him too much power and praise. He is a created being, nothing more. We sometimes fear him more than we fear God. There is something terribly wrong with that picture. It is for pride that he continues to try to get people to give him laud. Anytime his name is mentioned, he takes focus away from God and he (Satan) is glorified.

As you prepare yourself for prayer today, make sure your focus is on the Most High God. We have talked about the enemy, but don't focus on him. Spend adequate time praising the Lord God Almighty.

Today in your prayer time, I want you to cover three areas:

- Ask God to reveal any way that you have an exalted view of Satan in your life. Repent of what He shows you.

- Ask God to bring to mind any time or way you have been tricked into following the enemy—such as reading horoscopes, playing with an Ouija board, or watching TV programs that normalize and exalt the occult or paranormal.

- Ask God to show you any way you have tried to exalt yourself above others, get ahead of others, get better jobs, make more money, be right so someone else will be wrong, and so on. God can show you the specifics of how you might have tried to exalt yourself.

- Ask God to discern the thoughts and intents of your heart. Ask Him to show you any words you have said that reveal wrong motives in your heart. Ask Him to show you what has come out of your mouth that reveals vileness of your heart. Then be willing to accept what He says and repent if necessary. Ask Him to reveal what is in your heart that would cause you to have evil thoughts, murders (words can kill), adulteries (or thoughts of adultery), fornications, thefts, false witness, blasphemies. Ask Him to reveal your heart and cleanse you from all unrighteousness.

CHAPTER 4

Solitude: The Priority of Our Prayers

Mark 1:35 (NKJV)

[35]Now in the morning, having risen a long while before daylight, He went out and departed to a solitary place; and there He prayed.

Luke 5:16 (NKJV)

[16]So He Himself *often* withdrew into the wilderness and prayed.

Luke 9:18 (NKJV)

[18]And it happened, as He was alone praying, *that* His disciples joined Him, and He asked them, saying, "Who do the crowds say that I am?"

Matthew 14:23 (NKJV)

[23]And when He had sent the multitudes away, He went up on the mountain by Himself to pray. Now when evening came, He was alone there.

Matthew 6:6 (NKJV)

⁶But you, when you pray, go into your room, and when you have shut your door, pray to your Father who *is* in the secret *place;* and your Father who sees in secret will reward you openly.

How important is it to you that you get alone with God? The most common response is, "I just do not have the time." We each have the same amount of time each day: twenty-four hours are in every day. We are only different in how we choose to spend our 24 hours each day. You might say, "But you don't know all that I have to do." No, I do not know, but God does. I can assure you that God did not give you so much to do that you cannot spend quality time with Him. So then, who gave you all those things to do?

If God did not give you all of that stuff to do, who assigned you so many activities? Did you assign it to yourself? Did Satan? Did family members? God did not do it, that's for sure, because He desires for us to spend time alone with Him. He would never make us so busy that we couldn't have intimate fellowship with Him.

We assign ourselves things to do. Satan assigns things for us to do. Then we tell ourselves that we do not have time for being alone with God. As you can see from the Scriptures above, it is wise to spend time alone with God. It is simple really: if we do not "make time," time will make us. All of our time will be gone, and we will always wonder where the time went. Sometimes it seems that there is a vacuum that just consumes time. And if we do not spend priority time with God, we will inevitably feel frustrated because we did not get enough accomplished. The truth is the frustration comes because we have not had the priority of our soul met—Living Water and Bread of Life.

Why do you suppose Satan tries so hard to keep us too busy, too tired, or too distracted to pray? He knows better than we do what results when we spend time with the Father. He knows the *peace* that it produces within us. He knows the *power* that it releases in us. He knows the *manifest presence* of God that captivates us. Once you have been in God's presence, you will never be satisfied to be without His presence for too long a time. Being in God's presence energizes us!

How we spend our time reveals our priorities. Is it your priority to spend time alone with God? What would you rather do than be in

God's presence? Maybe it's not that you do not want to be in God's presence, maybe you do not know how to get there. I cannot imagine that once a person has experienced God's presence they would not want to be in His presence again and again.

How can we make prayer our priority? If your desire is not strong enough to make the needed commitment, pray that God will give you a strong desire and commitment to pray daily and consistently. Determine the best time for you to pray. The best time for you to pray may not be the most convenient time for you. It cannot be "leftover" time. The leftover time is often the dregs of our day. We do everything else we think we must do and *if* we have any time, we give that to God—maybe. That sounds like the children of Israel offering the animals that were blemished or sick. God was not pleased. I do not think He is pleased when we give Him the last drop of energy we have. That is a picture of praying from an attitude of duty and legalism, not from a loving, intimate relationship. I will pray because I must. Do you hear any joy in that praying?

The best time for you to pray will be the time of day when you are at your best. It is the time of day when you are making an offering of yourself to God. Remember that our offering to God needs to be the first and the best. In that time, we should offer ourselves as servants of the Most High and acknowledge His rule and reign over us.

Early morning may not be the majority of your prayer time, but it needs to be the first. You, as a servant of God, need to "report to work." Early morning prayer time sets the tone for the day. By bowing before God in early morning prayer, you acknowledge who has authority over your day. If you do not submit that authority to Him, you keep it to yourself, and we will always mess it up. By releasing it to Him, we can rest in His authority; have peace in knowing that He is in control of our day. Early each day we need to submit to the Lordship of Jesus and proclaim His greatness. Try this consistently for thirty days and see if there is a difference in your joy in praying.

Schedule your time alone with God. Schedule it within yourself as well as with you family. You will know that it is a committed time; it is your appointment time with God. Let your family know that this is a priority time and you are not available. Give your spouse the gift of a private priority time with God. During your spouse's time, answer the phone, keep the children busy, and so on. Protect your mate's time alone with God. You will also reap the benefit. Likewise, ask your spouse to do the same for you. Guard this time you have designated to be alone with God. It is the most important time of your day.

Keep your appointment with God even if you do not feel like it at first. Even if you do not sense God's presence in the beginning, keep your appointment with God anyway. Commit to meeting with God each and every day for at least thirty days. This appointment time will be a point of discipline for you, so meet with God each day, no matter what. And expect the enemy to try everything he can to distract you from the empowering, energizing effect of being in God's presence. After you have fought the battle of discipline, you will be amazed at how you begin to anticipate this time each day. It will become something that you simply do not want to live without. It will become the time for refreshing from the Bread of Life and the Living Water. And you will begin to hunger and thirst for more of Him.

Make this time a personal time: pray in secret. Your prayer closet can be any place of privacy. Collect your thoughts in one place. It is your responsibility to shut out all distractions. Shut the door and then pray! We should take responsibility to mentally shut out any distracting thoughts, feelings, attitudes, and so on. That is what it means to go into our closet and pray.

We need to be alone with God. It is not just a matter of wanting to be alone, we need alone time with Him. We need the priority of solitude with God. Jesus needed alone time with the Father, and so do you. Solitude with God happens when there is no longer anything before us except for God. Our thoughts are of Him, our focus is on Him, our attention is given to Him, and our devotion is toward Him. Our willingness to get alone with God shows our priority of prayer. I ask you to search your own heart to determine the priority you place on being alone with the loving God who redeemed you.

If we want to find an excuse, we can, and we will. If we really want time alone with God, we can, and we will find it. Jesus is waiting for fellowship with you. What takes priority in your life over that? The time spent with the Father will enrich your life. Search for the Lord with all of your heart, and He will be found. When we want Jesus more than anything else, that is when everything will fall into place.

Remember, we all have the same amount of time each day. How do you use it—what takes priority?

If you think that I am crazy, and you really cannot afford time alone with God, let me issue you a challenge. For one week, stick a notebook in your pocket and record how you spend your time. For example, *I hit the snooze button 4 times, I stood in the shower for 30 minutes trying to wake up, and I drank 3 cups of coffee. I watched the news. I ate breakfast for 15 minutes. I ate lunch for 30 minutes. I ate supper for 30 minutes. I watched the news for 1 hour. I washed dishes for 30 minutes. I swept the kitchen floor for 10 minutes. I watched TV for 2 hours to relax before bedtime. I took a nap in the afternoon for 45 minutes. I read the newspaper for 45 minutes.*

Tell me, which of these things would you present to God as a reason for not spending time alone with Him? Imagine that He is standing before you with His arms outstretched, wanting to have fellowship with you. Look into His eyes. Which reason do you want to extend to Him? What would you say?

Sometimes we live like God is not real. We live like He is only in our imagination. He is very real. He is standing with extended arms, wanting to have fellowship with His children, with you. "¹³And you will seek Me and find *Me,* when you search for Me with all your heart" (Jeremiah 29:13) (NKJV). When we want Him and His presence more than we want food and more than we want sleep, we will find Him.

SOLITUDE: THE PRIORITY OF OUR PRAYERS

Devotionals

Solitude: The Priority of Our Prayers

A Challenge to Pray

The first thing that I want to do is challenge you to get up earlier than usual, say thirty to forty-five minutes earlier than usual. Shower and dress and then get before the Lord in a private place. You might ask God the night before to meet you there at a particular time. Surely you can find some private place in your home. A friend and I used to pray in the bathroom. That was the only place that meant "stay out" when the door was closed. As I remember, it was a very small bathroom. I also remember some wonderful times when God showed up in a special way. At times, I have gone to the car to be alone with God. Somewhere to bow is preferable, but be willing to do what is necessary to meet alone with God. As you are kneeling before the Lord, read this verse aloud: "[17]I love those who love me, and those who seek me diligently will find me" (Proverbs 8:17) (NKJV).

Commit to God that you will meet Him there each morning this week. I wish that you would consider doing this for a month. It takes approximately thirty days of doing something consistently to form a habit. I hope the blessings of this week will motivate you to meet Him early each morning for years to come.

- Do you love Him—tell Him if you do.

- Tell Him that because you love Him, you are seeking Him early in the morning; you are diligently seeking Him by getting up early to be with Him.

- Tell Him you want to meet with Him at the same time each day this week; Tell Him that you will be there waiting for Him.

- Tell Him you want to get to know Him better.

- Ask Him to give you a greater desire to be with Him, especially the first thing each day.

This may be a test for some of you. That's okay. Do you want to know Him desperately enough to sacrifice to Him that last hour of sleep each morning for a week? I realize that it is hard when you are so tired and busy, but remember our priority of prayer.

I heard a story some time ago about a woman who decided that she needed to get up early to pray. Of course, she was very sleepy the next morning. As she tried to pray, she kept falling asleep. She was very sorrowful that she could not stay awake while she tried to pray. She determined to do better the next day. It went on like this for several days, and she simply could not make herself stay awake, even though she tried various things. Finally, she decided to stand on the edge of her bathtub while she prayed. That way, if she fell asleep, she would fall off of the bathtub and would awaken herself. That's what I call determination to pray.

As you make this new commitment, be prepared to be extra tired and sleepy. Be prepared for all sorts of distractions and interruptions. Remember, we need to make this appointment and keep it. If the commitment were getting to work on time, we would do whatever we needed to do to make sure that we got there on time. If the only time we could meet with the president of the United States was at 5:00 AM, we would be there with bells on. I have known people to get up at 3:00 AM to go stand in line for concert tickets for some rock-and-roll singer. What do you love enough to get up at 5:00 AM for? Is that love stronger than your love for Jesus? Spend time just loving on Him this morning. Get to know the sweetness of His presence.

Solitude: The Priority of Our Prayers

Search for God with All Your Heart

Jeremiah 29:13 (NKJV)

¹³**And you will seek Me and find *Me*, when you search for Me with all your heart.**

I know that we used this Scripture already in this chapter on solitude, but I want you to read it again and think about what it means to search for God with all of your heart. What do you want most in life? The idea of searching says that there is something important that is being sought. Have you ever lost something valuable or special to you? There is a moment of shock and panic when you realize it is missing. Then you begin looking everywhere you can think of to try and find it. You move furniture, tear apart beds, look outside in the grass, and so on. You look wherever you think you have been, retracing every step you can remember.

Think about the scenario that I just laid out for you. When you realize something priceless is missing and you are looking diligently to find it, you are, for the most part, unaware of anything else going on around you. You do not stop to enjoy the sunshine. You do not stop and casually smell the flowers. You do not even realize that you are hungry. You are on a mission; you are focused on a task. At that moment, nothing much matters to you other than finding that which is most important to you.

I think what God is saying in the Scripture from Jeremiah is that when we search for Him with such diligence that the importance of daily activities fade in comparison, we will find Him. When we search with all our heart for Him, we will seek Him and we will find Him! That sounds like a promise to me.

If you want to know more about this wonderful Holy God, search and seek with all of your heart, and He will find you while you are searching for Him.

As you prepare to pray today, do the previous things you have learned. Do not forget those. Once you have entered His presence, bask there awhile before asking Him anything. Tell Him how wonderful He is, and remind Him of all the good things He has done for you. You will be blessed, as He receives your praise.

- Ask Him to show you what you have been searching for that has left you empty.

- Ask Him to increase your desire to know Him.

- Ask Him to show you how to search for Him with all of your heart; do not stop until you find the priceless treasure of God Himself.

Solitude: The Priority of Our Prayers

Worth All They Owned

Matthew 13:44–46 (NKJV)

[44]"Again, the kingdom of heaven is like treasure hidden in a field, which a man found and hid; and for joy over it he goes and sells all that he has and buys that field." [45]"Again, the kingdom of heaven is like a merchant seeking beautiful pearls, [46]who, when he had found one pearl of great price, went and sold all that he had and bought it."

I realize that these verses are talking about the kingdom of heaven. Once we are saved, our place in heaven is secure. But, the kingdom of heaven has a ruler. That ruler is our Lord, Jesus Christ. Some say that the kingdom of heaven is among us; I really do not know about that. I do believe that the kingdom of *God* is within us. At any rate, I want us to think not about definitions but about the price that was paid. Notice in both of these parables the treasure was worth all that they owned.

Recently, a friend brought her baby by for a visit. I cannot describe the feeling I had when I looked into that precious baby's beautiful blue eyes and looked at her little round cheeks, not to mention her gorgeous auburn hair, those tiny fingers and toes, that sweet little cry. And oh, the feeling of feeding her and holding her while she slept. I did let my husband hold her for a few minutes. I looked over and saw a look of contentment on his face that I rarely, if ever, see.

After the visit was over and my heart was aching to hold her again, my husband jokingly but longingly asked, "Wonder how much they would take for her?" I responded, "I don't know, but we could offer them everything that we own." As the words came out of my mouth, the feeling in my heart was, "I would gladly give up everything to have her as my own. I would be happy to live in a dump and eat cornmeal mush just to have that precious little girl." I now think that I understand what grandparents feel when they see their precious grandchild.

Do we feel the same way about our Lord? Is He worth whatever it takes to obtain Him and His presence? What would you exchange? What would you give up to know Him better? Be prepared to offer it to Him. Today, ask yourself these questions as you prepare to pray. Pray that God will become most precious to you.

Solitude: The Priority of Our Prayers

Getting Alone with God: A Priority

Matthew 6:6 (NKJV)

⁶But you, when you pray, go into your room, and when you have shut your door, pray to your Father, who *is* in the secret *place*; and your Father who sees in secret will reward you openly.

What would it mean to be alone with God? Imagine that it is just you and God in the room where you are. Would you act any differently if He were literally sitting in a chair facing you? He is even closer than that, closer than you even know.

I said earlier that getting alone with God meant that there is nothing else before you except God; nothing else in your mind, nothing else in your heart but to know Him. Have you ever noticed that during prayer time some awful, very distracting thoughts can come into your mind? I think we all know where those come from. I have heard ministers talk about how a terrible sexual thought would often plague their minds, as they knelt to pray just before standing to preach a sermon. No one is exempt from the fiery darts of the enemy. Sometimes it is hard to go into your closet and shut the door behind you. Sometimes we literally have children knocking at the door. Even when we have the opportunity to be alone, it is difficult to shut the doors of our minds. We think about all we have to do, about how awful we feel, and many other things that distract us.

I acknowledge that getting alone with God is a difficult task. I also assure you that it is possible. The Lord directed us to do so, so it can be done. He knows the importance of being alone in His presence. He will help us get there if we want to be there badly enough. I have read stories about people who would literally get into a dark closet to pray. Do whatever you need to do to get alone with God.

As you prepare to pray today, I want you to consider some questions. Present them before your own heart and then to God. If there is something that needs to change related to these questions, deal with it before God today. If you are good in those areas—rejoice. Spend time thanking Him for His goodness and His mercy toward you—be specific.

Questions to consider:

- Are you willing to tell your family that you want this time alone with God?

- Are you willing to let the phone go unanswered? Who could possibly be more important to you than who you are already talking with?

- Are you willing to temporarily let things go undone at home to spend time alone with God? There are many things that will not matter a hundred years from now. The time you have spent alone with God will.

There is something special about being alone with the one that you love. It is time spent in intimacy, time looking into His eyes and telling Him how much you love Him. Do you want that today? If not, ask God to renew your love relationship with Him. Ask Him to show you how to have deeper intimacy with Him.

Solitude: The Priority of Our Prayers

Putting Things in Perspective

Matthew 14:22–23 (NKJV)

²²Immediately Jesus made His disciples get into the boat and go before Him to the other side, while He sent the multitudes away. ²³And when he had sent the multitudes away, He went up on the mountain by Himself to pray. Now when evening came, He was alone there.

Often we feel pulled in too many directions. Our family needs us, our friends need us, and we are also behind at work. That is not even counting the things we need to do at church. We just could not say no to all of those people who need us. That just would not be right, would it?

What did Jesus know that allowed Him to be able to send His best friends away? How could He send the multitudes of hurting people away? They were sick, and they were dying. They needed to know about salvation coming in the flesh, didn't they? Jesus was the only one who could heal them physically and spiritually. Didn't the disciples need to be learning from Him? After all, there was not that much time left.

In light of Jesus's behavior here in this passage of Scripture, I cannot help but think about our exaggerated sense of importance. We act as though if we do not do everything the world will fall apart. We have to dry every eye, wipe every nose, fix every problem, make sure the house is clean in case someone comes by, prepare a good supper, and in our spare time, we will work for the kingdom of God. God would not expect us to turn a deaf ear to someone in need would He? Jesus did.

I think what Jesus knew was that without the transformation that occurs in the Father's presence, He would not be ready to meet the needs. He recognized that what happens in God's presence is far more important than anything else He could do. He understood the value of spiritual strength and that it only comes from being in God's presence in prayer and the Word, anywhere God is found.

What I want you to see is that if Jesus knew it was okay to let some things go undone in order to be alone with the Father, it is okay for you to let some things go undone in order to be alone with the Father also. You cannot meet every need, but the more time that you spend alone with the Father, the more often you will know which need He wants to meet through you. Once you know what He wants you to do, you will have the strength and power to accomplish that task. If we try to do all these things in the flesh, we just burn out, because we are not empowered by His presence.

As you pray today, commit to God your willingness to get alone with Him even if things—what you consider important things—go undone. Ask Him to reveal the needs He wants to meet through you. Sometimes we try to rescue others from the fiery furnace when that is not our job. God may have allowed the trial for a specific purpose, and if we get people out of the situation too soon, they will only have to go through another trial later. We need to wait for God's direction in meeting the needs of others. We only need to worry about how we can get alone with Him so we can hear His sweet voice.

Prepare yourself to be in His presence. As you pray today:

- Ask God to show you ways that you have put doing things before being with Him.

- Ask Him to reveal your priorities to you. Repent if He has not been the top priority.

- Ask Him to show you how to change to make Him the top priority.

- Ask Him to show you the significance of being alone with Him versus meeting the needs that you see. Begin to praise God for being able to meet needs through you. Praise Him for being able to reveal the true needs that He wants to meet through you.

CHAPTER 5

Submission: The Reception of Our Prayers

Humility is an attitude of the heart; submission is the outward evidence of humility. Submission is the willingness to align ourselves in obedience to His commands. I believe we miss out on a lot God wants to give us because we fail to submit to His authority. Could the degree of our submission determine how much we receive from God in our prayers? Could it be that the degree of our submission is directly related to our degree of pride? Do we think we know better than God what should happen in a given situation? Are we too proud to admit our helplessness without Him? I would like to say that the safest and most productive place to be is under the umbrella of His authority. That is the place of joy.

There are several parts to submission. First, we acknowledge His rule over us. Second, we yield to that rule. Third, we listen for His voice. Fourth, we obey that rule and authority that He has over us. Fifth, we trust His rule.

Submission comes from the word "hupotasso," which is a military term meaning rank order. Consider some characteristics of a soldier that are common to a submitted Christian:

- Never his own boss

- Always under authority rule

- Dependent on God for direction

- Dependent on someone else for provision

- Absolutely filled with the commander's ways, wishes, and commands

- Disciplined for the work to be done

- Commander knows the dangers that others do not

- Soldier is taught to watch out for other soldiers

- Responsible for leadership and the care of those below their rank

- Responsible for particular things given to their care or guard

Why should we be submitted to God? Consider the following: when we submit to God, the responsibility of our lives goes to Him. He is responsible for my life—food, clothing, and so on, and He has a better plan for my life than I do. God sees the big picture even though I do not. He knows the plans and purpose He has for me, which I couldn't possibly know. He has more power and authority than I do. The payment plan and benefits are the absolute best. Security is absolute. I do not have to worry about stepping on a land mine if I obey His orders.

I think the concept of reception is twofold. First, submission to God's authority places us in a position that is easy for God to receive our prayers unto Himself. Second, submission allows us to receive God's response to our prayers.

Please read the following Scriptures:

Romans 8:19–22 (NKJV)
[19]For the earnest expectation of the creation eagerly waits for the revealing of the sons of God. [20]For the creation was subjected to futility, not willingly, but because of Him who subjected *it* in hope; [21]because the creation itself also will be delivered from the bondage of corruption into the

glorious liberty of the children of God. ²²Not only *that,* but we also who have the first fruits of the Spirit, even we ourselves groan within ourselves, eagerly waiting for the adoption, the redemption of our body.

1 Peter 2:18 (NKJV)

¹⁸Servants, *be* submissive to *your* masters with all fear, not only to the good and gentle, but also to the harsh.

Romans 13:1–7 (NKJV)

¹Let every soul be subject to the governing authorities. For there is no authority except from God, and the authorities that exist are appointed by God. ²Therefore whoever resists the authority resists the ordinance of God, and those who resist will bring judgment on themselves. ³For rulers are not a terror to good works, but to evil. Do you want to be unafraid of the authority? Do what is good, and you will have praise from the same. ⁴For he is God's minister to you for good, But if you do evil, be afraid; for he does not bear the sword in vain; for he is God's minister, an avenger to *execute* wrath on him who practices evil. ⁵Therefore *you* must be subject, not only because of wrath but also for conscience' sake. ⁶For because of this you also pay taxes, for they are God's ministers attending continually to this very thing. ⁷Render therefore to all their due: taxes to whom taxes *are due,* customs to whom customs, fear to whom fear, honor to whom honor.

1 Timothy 3:4 (NKJV)

⁴One who rules his own house well, having *his* children in submission with all reverence.

Ephesians 5:24 (NKJV)

²⁴Therefore, just as the church is subject to Christ, so *let the wives be* to their own husbands in everything.

Luke 10:17, 20 (NKJV)

¹⁷Then the seventy returned with joy, saying, "Lord, even the demons are subject to us in Your name."

20Nevertheless do not rejoice in this, that the spirits are subject to you, but rather rejoice because your names are written in heaven.

Hebrews 2:8 (NKJV)

8You have put all things in subjection under his feet. For in that He put all in subjection under him, He left nothing *that is* not put under him. But now we do not yet see all things put under him.

1 Corinthians 15:28 (NKJV)

28Now when all things are made subject to Him, then the Son Himself will also be subject to him who put all things under Him, that God may be all in all.

Jesus has the right to ask us to be in submission to Him; He earned it at Calvary. We are bought with a price; He redeemed us from the hand of the enemy. When we accept Christ as Savior, we accept the purchase price. We exchange lordship of our own lives for His Lordship. We are no longer our own; He is now the Master. That means that He is in control. He has the right to call all the shots of my life. I answer to Him.

All of those things are the truth, but we often fail to acknowledge that truth. We get saved and say, "I want you to redeem my soul from hell." Yet, we take back the control panel into our own hands. What does that have to do with prayer? Read the model prayer found in Matthew 6. When we pray, "Thy will be done," that is an act of submission.

When we pray, "Thy will be done," we are to submit to His Lordship. He is the Master, and we are to await His commands. We are to submit our will to His. When we say, "Your will, not mine," we are acknowledging His authority and His wisdom to know what is best. Consider some things we might want to submit to Him: our plans, our trust, our comfort, our material possessions, and our expectations, to name a few. If He is our sole authority, we must submit everything to Him.

Submission to His will also means learning to ask not to command or instruct God; we leave the options to Him. If we are not abiding under the umbrella of His authority and are off somewhere doing our own thing, I don't believe we are as likely to hear His instructions. Therefore, our degree of abiding at the point of submission greatly affects our joy and our effectiveness in prayer.

As stated before, our ability to hear God relates to our belief that He is God and that He is a rewarder of those who seek Him. We must be willing to humble ourselves before Him in order to hear Him. Our ability to hear God is directly related to our level of submission to authority as well as the degree of intimacy we share with Him.

There are several parts to submission. We must acknowledge His rule. We must yield to his rule. We must listen to His voice. We must trust Him. We must obey Him.

We sometimes tell God exactly how we want Him to answer our prayer. We tell Him the situation and then tell Him to do thus and such. When we tell Him what we want Him to do and He doesn't quickly obey us, we think He has failed to hear and answer. We need to remember who the Master is and who the servant is.

A private would not tell a general how to do battle. The private obeys commands; he does not give them. Isn't it funny that we think we know how to instruct the Creator of the universe? Talk about the clay telling the potter what to do. When we make a request or a petition of God, we need to, at that moment, submit that request to His Lordship.

We are free to say, "This is my need," and we can even tell Him what we would like to see happen, but we need to always leave it to His will. If we do not, we may find ourselves disillusioned, because He often does not answer the way we expected. We as humans find it easy to want something so badly that we can convince ourselves God will perform it a certain way. If we trust our own ideas instead of trusting His will, we can come away doubting God's love for us.

Listening is a part of prayer, yet I think this is a difficult area for most people. It is difficult to have a conversation if I cannot hear what you are saying. Willingness to hear is the first step to hearing, and that requires a submissive spirit. God really does still speak, but we often misinterpret what He says and that can be detrimental to us as well as to the church.

Sometimes God just speaks peace to our souls. Sometimes He gives us rhema words—the light is turned on when we read Scripture—we get it. Sometimes He speaks through a preacher or another believer, just saying something that hits your spirit. Sometimes you just know that you know something; it is so strong you cannot ignore it. Sometimes you can ask God a question, and the first thing that comes to your mind is His answer. Hearing His voice is still somewhat of a mystery; it is difficult for most people to discern. But the greater the intimacy, the less difficulty you will have in discerning His voice.

There have been several times in my life when the Lord spoke so clearly to my spirit there was no doubt who was speaking. I love those times. I wish it were always so clear. Even in those times, I do not completely understand. I know what He said, but I do not know exactly what He meant by it. Being human, we tend to filter what He says through human understanding and expectations.

We often leave all our requests at His feet and then we jump up and go on our way, without even waiting to hear if He wants to say something to us. That is pretty rude, don't you think? It is as if we really do not expect God to have anything to say to us. Is that true for you?

There have been times when I have finished praying that He has revealed something to me. Usually something I had no way of knowing except through divine revelation. For example, something that has happened somewhere else while I was praying and would later be confirmed. It was something I just knew in my spirit.

I have also had God just speak to my spirit and say, "I want to tell you something." Those special times will always be in my mind and heart.

Our ability to hear God is related to our belief that He is, and that He rewards those who diligently seek Him; our willingness to humble ourselves before Him; our level of submission to His authority; and the degree of intimacy we share with Him. All of these relate to our diligently seeking Him. Will you seek Him with your whole heart?

SUBMISSION: THE RECEPTION OF OUR PRAYERS

Devotionals

Submission: The Reception of Our Prayers

Submit and Resist

James 4:7 (NKJV)
⁷Therefore submit to God. Resist the devil and he will flee from you.

We read this Scripture at the beginning of the chapter, but we only touched on the first part—what it means to submit to God. Today, I want you to read this verse again and think about the entire verse. Why is submitting to God and resisting the Devil paired together?

Let's review a little. To submit to someone is to live under his authority or rule. James uses the term to describe someone who willingly and consciously chooses to submit to the Lordship of Jesus, who has the authority to be the Sovereign Ruler of the universe. This verse seems to suggest that we are to be active in the process of submitting and resisting.

I believe it is obvious James is assuming the reader already knows that a person is under the leadership of either God or Satan. There are no other options given. He does not give room for fence riding. You are either under submission to God's authority or to Satan's. We would like to think that there is some sort of middle ground. There isn't. You are either for God or you are against God. If you are against God, you are for Satan.

We would like to think that we are under our own authority at times. We seem to think if we are not under God's authority we can stand in the middle and wait awhile before making a final decision as to who to obey. We like to believe we can rule our own lives. To be very honest, in the past I have lived like this whole concept could be compared to a triangle. For the most part, I was master of my own life. In some instances, I knew God was leading me to do something, and

I decided to either to obey or disobey. Regardless, I was in control, I made the final decision, or so I thought.

Then there were times when I knew the things I did were not pleasing to God, but somehow I thought I had just temporarily withdrawn or withheld myself from God's authority or Lordship. I did not see it as bowing to the lordship of Satan. That thought is too serious for me, yet that is exactly what I was doing.

While writing this book, I was confronted with the truth that we are submitted to one or the other, not to our own authority. We are under someone's rule—and it is not our own. I believe God is going to bring this truth to a deeper level of acceptance within me. I suspect that it will change my life when it happens.

Today, I am going to ask you to read the entire fourth chapter of James. Pay especially close attention to the seventh verse.

As you pray today:

- Ask God to reveal His truth to you about this passage.

- Ask Him to reveal any time or any way that you submit to the Devil's authority instead of His.

- Ask God to show you if you have been a friend to the world.

- Ask Him to reveal any strong emotional attachment to this world's ways.

Look at the fourth verse. In order to be an adulterer, you must already be married to someone and then be unfaithful to them. That means that James must be addressing believers in Christ, who have already been given to His Lordship. He goes on to say that if we adopt the interests of the world to be our own, we are as an enemy to God. These are strong statements.

Have a blessed day in the Lord!

Submission: The Reception of Our Prayers

Our Bodies: Living Sacrifices

Romans 12:1 (NKJV)

¹I beseech you therefore, brethren, by the mercies of God, that you present your bodies a living sacrifice, holy, acceptable to God, *which* is your reasonable service.

This will be somewhat a follow-up to yesterday's devotional. The word "beseech" comes from the same word used when referring to the Holy Spirit. This word later came to mean to exhort or encourage. It is also used to mean counselor.

When Paul said, "therefore," he was referring to Romans 11:36: "For of Him and through Him and to Him *are* all things, to whom *be* glory forever. Amen." Paul was giving praise and glory to God. He was saying that all things are for God's glory. Therefore, we must also offer ourselves to be an instrument of His praise and glory.

Paul suggested that each of us should present our bodies as a living sacrifice as opposed to offering dead animals as sacrifices, as they had done in the past. Animal sacrifice is no longer necessary, because of what Jesus did at the cross. Because the penalty for sin was paid, the only sacrifice needed now is for an individual to offer oneself up completely to the Lord as a living sacrifice. We can then be used by the Lord as an instrument of righteousness.

Paul went on to say this is your, "reasonable service." Some translations say, "spiritual act of worship." Both of these terms mean the same thing. Paul was saying that since everything is for His glory and His mercies are so great, it is only logical that we offer ourselves up as a living sacrifice.

The second verse says, "Do not be conformed." Paul is talking about assuming an outward appearance or expression that does not reflect the true inward nature. Of course, "this world" means the ideas, beliefs, values, and so on, of the present age. Paul was saying do not try to fit in with the crowd. Do not act like everyone else. What you are on the inside is who you really are, no matter what image we try to project on the outside. Let who you really are on the inside show. Be who you are in Christ at all times. Who you really are is what the Scripture says you are—that is truth.

Paul went on to say, "Be transformed." This Greek word is where we get our word "metamorphosis." It means to have a change in outward appearance. The same word is used of Jesus's transfiguration. His outward appearance changed, as He was in the presence of the Father. Moses' outward appearance also changed when He was in God's presence. Jesus briefly displayed outwardly his inner divine nature. Paul was encouraging the Roman Christians to show outwardly their divine, redeemed nature, which was on the inside.

Paul said that this kind of transformation only occurs by, "the renewing of the mind." It comes as the Holy Spirit changes our thinking through study of the Scripture. A renewed mind is one that is controlled and filled with God's Word. May I add that I think the more we are in God's presence the more we are transformed into His likeness. This sacrifice is the one that Paul says is acceptable to God.

May I suggest to you today that in your prayer time you present your body as a living sacrifice, completely yielding to God in service.

- Thank Him that the Holy Spirit will come alongside each one of us to encourage and strengthen us.

- Thank Him for His great mercies.

- Ask God to show you ways that you have conformed to this world's ways.

- Ask Him to reveal ideas, beliefs, and values that are not His but the world's.

- Ask Him to help you manifest your inner divine nature to those around you. In other words, act like who you really are.

- Ask Him to transform you by the renewing of your mind.

- Commit to renewing your mind through studying His Word and spending time in His presence.

Submission: The Reception of Our Prayers

A Servant's Heart

1 Peter 2:18–21 (NKJV)

¹⁸Servants, *be* **submissive to** *your* **masters with all fear, not only to the good and gentle, but also to the harsh. ¹⁹For this is commendable, if because of conscience toward God one endures grief suffering wrongfully. ²⁰For what credit is it if, when you are beaten for your faults, you take it patiently? But when you do good and suffer, if you take it patiently, this is commendable before God. ²¹For to this you were called, because Christ also suffered for us, leaving us an example, that you should follow His steps.**

Ephesians 6:5–9 (NKJV)

⁵Bondservants, be obedient to those who are your masters according to the flesh, with fear and trembling, in sincerity of heart, as to Christ; ⁶not with eyeservice, as men-pleasers, but as bondservants of Christ, doing the will of God from the heart, ⁷with goodwill doing service, as to the Lord, and not to men, ⁸knowing that whatever good anyone does, he will receive the same from the Lord, whether *he is* **a slave or free. ⁹And you, masters, do the same things to them, giving up threatening, knowing that your own Master also is in heaven, and there is no partiality with Him.**

We don't like to think of ourselves as servants. That concept touches our rebellious nature. Yet, if we are in a public job, we are to a degree a servant of that company or person. Keep in mind we are discussing the idea of submission. Submission means to, "align ones self under some other authority." When we are working outside the home, we are under someone else's authority. We must do what the higher authority expects us to or we will be fired.

Some are fortunate enough to have jobs with a kind master. Others are not so fortunate. Some people go to jobs each day where they are treated with disrespect and contempt; others do not.

The passages of Scripture from 1 Peter and Ephesians teach us that God realizes that some have harsh masters or bosses. These masters or bosses will one day answer to Him for the treatment that they gave His servants. God commanded His people to obey and submit even to the harsh masters.

Ephesians teaches us to obey as to Christ with sincerity of heart. We are to submit from a sincere heart, not just outwardly, while inwardly hating every minute of it. We must watch carefully our attitudes and our grumblings. I think the key to being able to submit to something or to someone you know is wrong is remembering that God is our rewarder, or true Master. Ephesians teaches us that whatever good we do; we will receive the same from the Lord. I would rather have the good He gives than all the perks of any job.

Today, as you pray:

- Ask God to reveal your true attitude about your masters in the workforce.

- Ask Him to give you a servant's heart toward them, seeing clearly their need.

- Ask Him to remove any resentment or bitterness toward your earthly masters.

- Ask Him to show you how to do well in your situation.

- Ask God how to pray for your bosses and then pray as He directs. Ask Him to continue to lead you to pray for their true needs.

Don't forget to praise Him. Maybe you want to thank Him for providing your job. Thank Him if you have a kind boss. Ask Him to use you as a witness if you have a harsh one.

Submission: The Reception of Our Prayers

Subject to the Governing Authority

Romans 13:1–7 (NKJV)

¹Let every soul be subject to the governing authorities. For there is no authority except from God, and the authorities that exist are appointed by God. ²Therefore whoever resists the authority resists the ordinance of God, and those who resist will bring judgment on themselves. ³For rulers are not a terror to good works, but to evil. Do you want to be unafraid of the authority? Do what is good, and you will have praise form the same. ⁴For he is God's minister to you for good. But if you do evil, be afraid; for he does not bear the sword in vain; for he is God's minister, an avenger to *execute* wrath on him who practices evil. ⁵Therefore *you* must be subject, not only because of wrath but also for conscience sake. ⁶For because of this you also pay taxes, for they are God's ministers attending continually to this very thing. ⁷Render therefore to all their due: taxes to whom taxes *are due,* customs to whom customs, fear to whom fear, honor to whom honor.

1 Peter 2:13–17 (NKJV)

¹³Therefore submit yourselves to every ordinance of man for the Lord's sake, whether to the king as supreme, ¹⁴or to governors, as to those who are sent by him for the punishment of evildoers and *for the* praise of those who do good. ¹⁵For this is the will of God, that by doing good you may put to silence the ignorance of foolish men—¹⁶as free, yet not using liberty as a cloak or vice, but as bondservants of God. ¹⁷Honor all *people.* Love the brotherhood. Fear God. Honor the king.

These two passages are talking about being submitted or subject to the governing authorities of the land. In other words, we are to obey the laws that the government establishes. Romans 13:1 teaches us that whoever is in authority, God has appointed for a purpose. Yes, that includes the evil ones. I am not suggesting that if the government told you to do something that was in stark opposition to God's laws that we should immediately go out and obey. I do think these passages are teaching that governing bodies are established for our protection, not our harm. Laws are intended to keep order. There it is again, that reference to rank order, that submission word.

To me, one of the most important ideas being conveyed in these passages is that of being held blameless by the world. Both Peter and Paul are urging Christians to live in such a manner that unbelievers could not accuse them of evildoing. How many times have we heard someone ask, "Did you see what they were doing or hear what they said? Those people are supposed to be Christians." Does that mean you as a Christian are supposed to abide strictly by the law? Yes, that is exactly what it means. "But everybody does it. Nobody even thinks anything about it; can't I do it, too?" No, you cannot and still be obedient to these commands.

Paul pointed out one area he knew we fine Christians would have a problem with: paying our taxes. We often think, *preaching about money is nothing more than meddling.* I know it is hard to give so much of your hard-earned money away to a government that wastes more than it uses. I hate it, too. But yes, it means we are to be totally honest with our taxes.

What about abiding by the speed limit? That is the law, isn't it? Please hear me, I am not preaching. I speed sometimes myself, but I do know better. Several years ago, while doing a Precept Bible Study, the Lord convicted me of so many things I couldn't possibly tell them all. Speeding was one of them, so I can tell you without hesitation, it is wrong. On the occasion that I now break the speed limit, I am always reminded of my sin by the precious Holy Spirit. Let the Lord show you what He showed me. You probably will not be convinced until you hear His voice. He has a lot more authority than I do.

Don't forget to prepare to pray—acknowledge His authority, His holiness, and so on. By now, you know when you are in the attitude of prayer.

As you pray today:

- Always begin with thanksgiving and praise.

- Thank God we have laws and rules in our country, if not, everyone would be doing what is right in their own eyes—a recipe for trouble.

- Ask God to bring to your mind any way in which you are not submitting to the governing authorities—such as breaking the law or being disrespectful to your rulers.

- Ask Him to show you if you have done things that have brought discredit to His Holy Name, since you also carry the name of Christ.

- Pray that He will convict you in the future when you break the law or do something that is displeasing to His name.

Submission: The Reception of Our Prayers

Submissive Husbands and Wives

1 Peter 3:1–7 (NKJV)

¹Wives, likewise, *be* submissive to your own husbands, that even if some do not obey the word, they, without a word, may be won by the conduct of their wives, ²when they observe your chaste conduct *accompanied* by fear. ³Do not let your adornment be *merely* outward—arranging the hair, wearing gold, or putting on *fine* apparel—⁴rather *let it be* the hidden person of the heart, with the incorruptible *beauty* of a gentle and quiet spirit, which is very precious in the sight of God. ⁵For in this manner, in former times, the holy women who trusted in God also adorned themselves, being submissive to their own husbands, ⁶as Sarah obeyed Abraham, calling him lord, whose daughters you are if you do good and are not afraid with any terror. ⁷Husbands, likewise, dwell with *them* with understanding, giving honor to the wife, as to the weaker vessel, and as *being* heirs together of the grace of life, that your prayers may not be hindered.

Ephesians 5:22–33 (NKJV)

²²Wives, submit to your own husbands, as to the Lord. ²³For the husband is head of the wife, as also Christ is head of the church; and He is the Savior of the body. ²⁴Therefore, just as the church is subject to Christ, so *let* the wives *be* to their own husbands in everything. ²⁵Husbands, love your wives, just as Christ also loved the church and gave Himself for her, ²⁶that He might sanctify and cleanse her with the washing of water by the word, ²⁷that He might present her to Himself a glorious church, not having spot or wrinkle or any such things, but that she should be holy and without blemish. ²⁸So husbands

ought to love their own wives as their own bodies; he who loves his wife loves himself. ²⁹For no one ever hated his own flesh, but nourishes and cherishes it, just as the Lord *does* the church. ³⁰For we are members of His body, of His flesh and of His bones. ³¹"For this reason a man shall leave his father and mother and be joined to his wife, and the two shall become one flesh." ³²This is a great mystery, but I speak concerning Christ and the church. ³³Nevertheless let each one of you in particular so love his own wife as himself, and let the wife *see* that she respects *her* husband.

Now, you did not really think that we would get out of this submission devotional without at least one reference to wives and husbands did you? Be encouraged. God's ideas are good for us, even these.

Let me say right up front that we will not be looking at the husband's role in depth. So, keep in mind that the other half has not been told. That is a lesson for another time.

Notice that the first thing both writers said was, "Wives be submissive to your own husband." If a man, any man, treats a woman as a husband ought to, the woman has a tendency to want to respond to him as a wife. Many affairs have started because some man made a woman feel "special" or "cherished" or "loved" or "protected" or "taken care of." That is all it took: she was hooked. The woman finds herself responding whether she planned to or not. Actually, women need to be very cautious in the workplace. It is an ideal place for affairs to get started. What the woman doesn't realize is the man who makes her feel so "special" does not treat his wife that way—and would not treat her that way if she were his wife.

So, I believe these writers are saying, "Women, be very careful that you only respond to or submit to your own husband." In thinking about the meaning of submission, "living under the authority of," it occurs to me that, since men naturally have a more authoritative demeanor, it would also be natural for a woman to submit to his authority. That seems to be true everywhere except within our marriages. Why is that?

You have to look back at the book of Genesis to find the answer. After the fall, God spoke to the couple and explained the consequences of their choices. In Genesis 3:16, God told Eve she would have an increase in sorrow and conception. In pain, she would bring forth children. Personally, I think God meant more than the pain of childbirth. What gives a mother more pain than grieving over her children, regardless of their age?

The last part of the sixteenth verse in Genesis 3 says, "Your desire shall be for your husband, and he will rule over you." Now read Genesis 4:7. Here God is talking to Cain, "Sin lies at your door and its desire for you, but you should rule over it." The Hebrew word for desire is the same in both verses. It is obvious that God is saying that sin wanted to overtake Cain and rule over him. Do you see the connection? Part of the curse on Eve was that there would be something inside her that wanted to rule her husband, but it would not happen because God has ordained it be another way. Therefore, man and woman will face struggles in their relationships with each other as husband and wife. There will be a struggle between the couple related to self-will and the desire to rule.

Each time I read these passages, I am reminded of God's goodness, and I am so thankful. The Lord revealed this truth to me approximately twenty years ago. I began teaching it and using it in marriage counseling situations. It has only been the last few years that I have read other commentaries that bring out the same point. That is a wonderful confirmation of what God revealed to me.

I believe that this struggle is the basis of most, if not all, marital problems. Christian women want their husbands to lead but to get out of the way when he does not lead like she thinks he should. Over and over I have heard women say the thing they want more than anything is for the husband to "lead," while the husband states he wants to lead but can't because she won't let him. I think that we would be amazed if God would open our eyes to see how all of this really plays out in our daily lives.

We are not going to go any deeper into the teaching on wives and husbands. Let me just point out that wives are to be subject to their husbands, just as the church is to Christ. The church is trusting Christ to keep His promises—to provide, to protect, and to care for the church. Wives are to do the same with their husbands. Sadly, many husbands do not pick up their end of the responsibility. Husbands and wives, may I challenge you to find a place in Scripture that will let you off of the hook for your end of the deal, even if your spouse does not obey the Word.

As you pray today, humble yourself before Him.

- Ask God to reveal to you how you struggle with your spouse for self-will.

- Ask Him to reveal ways that you are not being a submissive wife who honors her husband or a husband who does not care for, protect, cherish, and provide for his wife.

- Ask Him to reveal any dangers of submitting to some other man who treats you in a way only your husband should. Or maybe you are the man who treats the lady at work the way you should be treating only your wife.

- Thank God for your spouse. Think of at least ten things you are thankful for related to your spouse (comes home at night, works, is a good parent, loves God, and goes to church).

CHAPTER 6

Forgiveness: The Freedom of Our Prayers

Matthew 6:12, 14–15 (NKJV)

¹²**And forgive us our debts, as we forgive our debtors.**
¹⁴**For if you forgive men their trespasses, your heavenly
Father will also forgive you.** ¹⁵**But if you do not forgive
men their trespasses, neither will your Father forgive
your trespasses.**

1 John 1:9 (NKJV)

⁹**If we confess our sins, He is faithful and just to forgive
us *our* sins and to cleanse us from all unrighteousness.**

What does forgiveness have to do with our prayer life? We must be
forgiven and accepted in the Beloved before we can have an effective
prayer life or have any measure of joy in praying. That kind of forgiveness
is not what we will be talking about. We are going to be talking about
forgiving one another and how that affects our prayers.

When Jesus was teaching the disciples how to pray, He included
the issue of forgiveness. Let it be understood that this is not saying

that you lose your salvation if you do not forgive others. Salvation is a permanent and complete pardon from the guilt and penalty of sin.

The Scripture teaches that believers are to confess their sins quickly for a spiritual cleansing from the world's defilements of sin. It is the way we stay current with the Lord; we do not allow our failures to cling to us. We release them to the Lord, and He, in turn, releases us from the guilt and shame.

Let's look at what the word "forgive" means. Forgive means to send forth or away, to let go from oneself. It means to let go from one's power, possession, to let go free, let escape, or to let go from obligation toward oneself. To "forgive sins" is to remove the sins from someone. Only God can do that. To forgive sins is not to disregard them and do nothing about them. It is to liberate a person from them, their guilt, and their power. When we ask God to forgive us our sins, we are asking Him to remove them from us. We ask Him to remove them from us so that we do not stand guilty and are not under their power any longer.

We do not have the power to forgive sins toward God. He alone has the power and authority to do so. We are, however, expected to forgive things done to us. This means we are to let go of the offense and to send it away from us. We are to let it go and not give any further attention to it. We should no longer be occupied with the offense; we have let it go.

> **Romans 12:17–21 (NKJV)**
>
> ¹⁷**Repay no one evil for evil. Have regard for good things in the sight of all men. ¹⁸If it is possible, as much as depends on you, live peaceably with all men. ¹⁹Beloved, do not avenge yourselves, but *rather* give place to wrath; for it is written, *"Vengeance is Mine, I will repay,"* says the Lord. ²⁰Therefore *"If your enemy is hungry, feed him; if he is thirsty, give him a drink; for in so doing you will heap coals of fire on his head." ²¹Do not be overcome by evil but overcome evil with good.**

To me, these verses are saying that until we release it, God does not move in the situation. Once we release it to God through forgiveness, He will repay. That should give us some comfort in forgiving those who have injured us deeply. Already, you can see how refusing to forgive can block our prayers.

Matthew 18:21–35 (NKJV)

²¹Then Peter came to Him and said, "Lord, how often shall my brother sin against me, and I forgive him? Up to seven times?" ²²Jesus said to him, "I do not say to you, up to seven times, but up to seventy times seven. ²³Therefore the kingdom of heaven is like a certain king who wanted to settle accounts with his servants. ²⁴And when he had begun to settle accounts, one was brought to him who owed him ten thousand talents. ²⁵But as he was not able to pay, his master commanded that he be sold, with his wife and children and all that he had, and that payment be made. ²⁶The servant therefore fell down before him, saying, 'Master, have patience with me, and I will pay you all.' ²⁷Then the master of that servant was moved with compassion, released him, and forgave him the debt. ²⁸But that servant went out and found one of his fellow servants who owed him a hundred denarii; and he laid hands on him and took him by the throat, saying, 'Pay me what you owe!' ²⁹So his fellow servant fell down at his feet and begged him, saying, 'Have patience with me, and I will pay you all' ³⁰And he would not, but went and threw him into prison till he should pay the debt. ³¹So when his fellow servants saw what had been done, they were very grieved and came and told their master all that had been done. ³²Then his master, after he had called him, said to him, 'You wicked servant! I forgave you all that debt because you begged me. ³³Should you not also have had compassion on your fellow servant, just as I had pity on you?' ³⁴And his master was angry, and delivered him to the torturers until he should pay all that was due to him. ³⁵So My heavenly Father also will do to you if each of you, from his heart, does not forgive his brother his trespasses."

This Scripture teaches us that the Heavenly Father will turn us over to the tormentor if we do not forgive our brother his trespass against us. These verses also show us how much greater our sin was to Jesus than anything a brother could do to us. He is saying that if He could forgive such a debt, one that could never be repaid, how can we withhold forgiveness regarding things that are only temporal?

This Scripture also teaches that our fellowship with God can be hindered by a broken fellowship with our brother. For example, when we are angry at our spouse, it is difficult to feel joy in prayer or pray effectively. We need to submit that offense and release it to God's judgment before we can find the freedom to pray or hear God. We can be assured that God is just and sees all offenses done to us as well as those that we do to others. He really will take care of things. Our job is to forgive, even when we don't feel like we can. There have been times I have had to pray, "God I am so hurt I cannot forgive, please give me Your grace to forgive," and He has.

We struggle with true forgiveness. Since forgiveness is sending it away and not being occupied with the offense, I suspect many of us have forgiveness issues to deal with. As long as we refuse to forgive, we are tormented by it, because we are often consumed and controlled by our unresolved feeling. Refusing to forgive is sin, therefore, until we choose to forgive others, our own sin and guilt cannot be sent away from us. We will have the guilt and power of it attached to us in some form or fashion. We will be preoccupied with the offense and the person who offended us. We are tied to that person through our emotions whether we want to be or not. According to the above Scriptures, our offerings or prayers to God are greatly affected until forgiveness occurs. Then, our prayers can freely flow from our heart to God's, and joy can again fill our life. In addition, as long as we withhold forgiveness from our brother, we block the wrath of God in that person's life.

Forgiveness frees us from the offense as well as from the person. As mean as someone may have been to us, as long as we think about the person and the offense, we are attached to them; they occupy a major part of our thoughts and feelings. Forgiveness frees us to pray for that person as well as to bless them. Forgiveness frees us to make our offering to God. Forgiveness frees us to act in our Father's nature—we forgive as we have been forgiven. We are never more like the Father than when we forgive. Forgiveness frees us to accept others as fallible human beings. Forgiveness also frees us from extreme expectations, which, in turn, can free us from further hurt.

We need to ask forgiveness for our debts because it restores fellowship. Debt is not the same thing as an offense. Debt is something owed or an obligation. After you offend someone, you owe them an apology. Once you do something wrong, you need to make restitution for the offense. It is the consequences of the offense, it is the debt owed.

To forgive a debtor is to release them from the consequences of their actions. They do not owe you anything more. Isn't that what was given to us through the gift of grace? After accepting Jesus as Savior, we are released from the consequences of our sins, which was death.

According to the *Complete Word Study Dictionary*, the word translated "trespasses" in Matthew 18:35 is often used where pardon is mentioned and is talking about a fault that is not necessarily desperately wicked. So, the trespasses and forgiveness being referred to are not talking about salvation. It is referring to a person's weaknesses or faults. I think it is saying that if you forgive, the power of the offense will be sent away from the one having been offended, and in addition, the offended person is now in a position to be released from the power and guilt of his own offenses toward others.

To sum up, if we cannot release our own sin, maybe it is because we are withholding forgiveness toward someone else. As long as we refuse to forgive, we are tormented by the offense and the person. Our own guilt and sin cannot be sent away from us. We will have the guilt and power of it attached to us. We may even have bitterness attached to us. We are preoccupied with the offense and the person who offended us, and we are tied to that person through emotions. Our offerings or prayers to God are greatly hindered until forgiveness occurs. Once forgiveness is given, our prayers and our joy are then free. We block the wrath of God in the other person's life. We block His correction, discipline, and so on, for that person.

Forgiveness is so important that Jesus taught we should leave our offering at the altar, go take care of the issue, and then come back and do business with Him. That sounds to me like an urgent issue.

Forgiveness from God and Jesus Christ for our sins is what begins our life as Christians. We must ask for forgiveness and be washed in the blood of Jesus Christ to be clean. He gave His life for you and me and paid for our past, present, and future sins. Comparatively speaking, it should be really easy for us to forgive someone who has said something that hurt our pride or even some greater offense. Do we trust God to be a just God? Do we really trust that He loves us and is our Good Shepherd?

FORGIVENESS: THE FREEDOM OF OUR PRAYERS

Devotionals

Forgiveness: The Freedom of Our Prayers

Reconciliation

Matthew 5:23–24 (NKJV)
²³Therefore if you bring your gift to the altar, and there remember that your brother has something against you, ²⁴leave your gift there before the altar, and go your way. First be reconciled to your brother, and then come and offer your gift.

Have you ever done something to someone that maybe was not "all that bad," but you were embarrassed that you did it? Maybe you feel so bad that you avoid them if you see them in the store. You get sick at your stomach when you accidentally run into them. You want to duck your head and turn invisible at that moment.

At this moment, I cannot remember what I did, but I can remember that feeling of shame on several occasions. We all know the feeling of having done something we know is not right toward another person and wishing we had done things differently. We think that it is too late, the damage is already done. The only thing we can do is avoid the person for the rest of our life. Well, there is something else you can do. You can confess your fault to the other person and ask them for forgiveness. That puts the ball in the other person's court. You have done what is required of you.

The Scripture for today talks about being reconciled before you come back to your offering. According to *The Complete Word Study Dictionary*, the word translated reconcile indicates it really does not matter which of the two parties is at fault, just that there is a break in the relationship. So, this would also apply regardless of which person was at fault. As a matter of fact, in most instances, both parties are somewhat at fault. In many cases, a misunderstanding can either create lifelong friction or an opportunity to deepen a relationship.

When the above Scripture talks about being reconciled, I believe it is referring to changing your feelings toward someone. Have you ever noticed that when we get offended toward someone, we can get rather stubborn in our unwillingness to look objectively at the situation? To look at a situation objectively requires that we also examine our own motives and actions. This entire process requires submission of our prideful selves to God as well as to the other person. To be willing to submit for the greater cause of reconciliation expresses an element of dying to self and taking up the cross and following Jesus. He is all about reconciling sinners to Himself.

Remember to prepare yourself for prayer today. Revere His holiness and begin by thanking and praising the only One worthy of praise. As you pray today:

- Ask God to reveal any broken relationships that He wants to reconcile. Be careful that it is His leadership and not a false sense of guilt.

- Ask Him to search your heart and bring to your remembrance any brother or sister you have offended and need to ask for their forgiveness.

- Thank Him that He forgives both you and the other party.

Forgiveness: The Freedom of Our Prayers

Unconfessed Sin and Forgiveness

Matthew 6:12 (NKJV)
¹²And forgive us our debts, as we forgive our debtors.

Think about what an offense or sin does to us, the guilt and shame we feel, the distance we feel toward God. We are eager to be rid of the feeling, though we are sometimes reluctant to deal with the issue before God. Have you ever noticed how understanding we are of our own sins and the sins of those closest to us? We are quick to hope our consequences are light to none. But it is often a different story when it comes to someone else, especially if we don't like that person very much. We can be downright harsh in our judgment of deliberate sin as well as unintentional faults and failures.

The above Scripture suggests a proper way to pray is to ask God to forgive us as we forgive. How do you forgive? Are you quick to forgive? Do you freely release things, or do you have to grapple with it for a period of time until they have suffered awhile? Do you bring it back up over and over, or is the offense cast away from your memory? Would you ask God to forgive you in the same manner as you have forgiven your worst offender?

Get quiet before God with your Bible open to this passage. Meditate on these words before beginning your prayer. When you are ready:

- Ask God to bring to your mind any unconfessed sin that has caused a break in your fellowship with Him.

- Ask Him to cleanse you right now.

- Ask Him to reveal your secret sins to you right now, the motives of your heart.

- Ask God to reveal and remind you of those things you struggle with in your life, those things that keep tripping you up as a Christian. Ask Him to reveal those things that you have tried and tried to win the victory over, only to fail again.

- Ask God to cause you to feel Godly sorrow so that you might readily repent and receive His forgiveness.

- Ask Him to cause you to feel the release of His cleansing within you. As we discussed yesterday, guilt and shame will cause you to want to avoid God also. We just feel so much better when we have confessed our failures to the Father. Thank God, that failure is not final.

- Ask God to help you forgive as He has forgiven you—quickly, freely, and completely.

- Ask God to bring to mind anyone who needs your forgiveness today.

Forgiveness: The Freedom of Our Prayers

Remembering His Goodness

Luke 7:36–48 (NKJV)

[36]Then one of the Pharisees asked Him to eat with him. And He went to the Pharisee's house, and sat down to eat. [37]And behold, a woman in the city who was a sinner, when she knew that *Jesus* sat at the table in the Pharisee's house, brought an alabaster flask of fragrant oil, [38]and stood at His feet behind *Him* weeping; and she began to wash His feet with her tears, and wiped *them* with the hair of her head; and she kissed His feet and anointed *them* with the fragrant oil. [39]Now when the Pharisee who had invited Him saw *this,* he spoke to himself, saying, "This man, if He were a prophet, would know who and what manner of woman *this is* who is touching Him, for she is a sinner." [40]And Jesus answered and said to him, "Simon, I have something to say to you." So he said, "Teacher, say it." [41]"There was a certain creditor who had two debtors. One owed five hundred denarii, and the other fifty. [42]And when they had nothing with which to repay, he freely forgave them both. Tell Me, therefore, which of them will love him more?" [43]Simon answered and said, "I suppose the *one* whom he forgave more." And He said to him, "You have rightly judged." [44]Then He turned to the woman and said to Simon, "Do you see this woman? I entered you house; you gave Me no water for My feet, but she has washed My feet with her tears and wiped *them* with the hair of her head. [45]You gave Me no kiss, but his woman has not ceased to kiss My feet since the time I came in. [46]You did not anoint My head with oil, but this woman has anointed My feet with fragrant oil. [47]Therefore I say to you, her sins, *which are* many, are forgiven, for she loved much. But to whom

little is forgiven, *the same* **loves little." ⁴⁸Then He said to her, "Your sins are forgiven."**

We have already talked about those little "not so bad" things we do. Today we want to think about those things we consider being major. Incredibly, some of you have never committed those major sins. Some of you were saved at an early age and have remained faithful to your Master. I commend you for your faithfulness.

On the other hand, there are those who have lived as if they did not know the Lord as Savior. Many have temporarily forsaken their commitment to the Father and forgotten promises made. Thankfully, many have at a later date returned to their first love and then had to live with their past spiritual adultery. I have heard so many agonize over the feeling of, "I cannot believe I did that."

Perhaps some of you have done horrible things, things you would rather not even think about. But we do think about them; they haunt us. Be assured that there is nothing you could have done, thought, or felt that would change God's heart toward you. I am not suggesting our sins are minor or unimportant to God. I am suggesting He is bigger. I am suggesting He will graciously forgive you and cleanse you.

The Scripture for today's reading is encouraging to those who have been entangled in some failure. This woman was probably a well-known prostitute. Apparently Simon the Pharisee either knew her personally or knew her reputation. Either way, you can hear the disrespect in his tone. He thought she was "less than" he.

This woman came boldly to see Jesus. It would have been a disgrace for a woman to enter a house where a group of men were gathered, especially a woman of her reputation. She wept at His presence. Her tears washed His feet. She dried them with her hair, another unheard of thing. A woman only let her hair down in private, never in public. To let one's hair down was a sign of intimacy. She brought an alabaster flask of fragrant oil to His feet. This flask of oil was probably what this woman had saved for all her life for her own burial. It represented a lot of money that had been cautiously saved over the years. Think about the amount of life insurance you have. Would you love the Lord enough to wash His feet with something of that value? The washing of His feet to some would have seemed like a waste, because in a few minutes, it would be gone, and what good did it do anyway?

It was an expression of her love for Him. Do you love Him enough to pour at His feet all that you have saved, all that you plan to use for your future? The Pharisees thought Jesus would not allow such a woman to touch Him. They did not realize that it was for those like her that He came.

Jesus told the Pharisees those who are forgiven much, love much. Are you one of those people? Truly, our sin nature is worse than filthy rags, and that alone is more than enough for us to rejoice over. But, there are those people who have a magnified perception of the results of their sin nature due to past or present behavior. Jesus said those who have been forgiven much, love much. We all have been forgiven much, but those with the magnified perception of their sinfulness also have a greater awareness of the depths from which they have come.

I love ice cream. It is as if all of my family has ice cream flowing through our veins instead of blood. Ice cream at my house has been a daily thing for as far back as I care to remember. At least it has been in my adult years. Several weeks ago, I quit ice cream cold turkey. Since I have diabetes, I have to watch the carbohydrates that I eat. I thought I would give up ice cream to improve my blood-sugar levels as well as my weight problem. I have done rather well; I have not sneaked any and have not bought any and brought it into the house.

Last night, after church, I decided I would have a bowl of ice cream. I stopped by the store and bought my favorite kind, Blue Bunny Tin Roof Sundae. I let it soften a little, just the way I like it. I filled my special ice cream bowl, yes I have one, and sat down to enjoy. I cannot tell you the satisfaction of that ice cream. It had been weeks since I had tasted that special smoothness.

As I thought about how much I was enjoying the ice cream, I thought about how I had become accustomed to the taste and richness when I was eating it every day. I was not nearly so aware of its goodness then. It was only when it was not present for a while that I truly came to appreciate the taste of ice cream.

I think the same thing is true about what Jesus said to the Pharisees. Only those who have been far away from His presence can truly appreciate His goodness. That is not to suggest that you should deliberately go into sin to appreciate Him more. The story of the prodigal son teaches us that we should not. When the brother who stayed home became angry, the father said, "All that I have is yours." It was not the father who loved more; it was the prodigal son, because he had an increased awareness of his father's goodness.

Today as you pray:

- Thank God for His goodness toward you.

- Make a list of this goodness, and thank Him for each thing.

- Thank God for His forgiveness toward those of us who have "gone far away" and committed the "major sins."

- Sit at His feet, wipe them with your tears, and dry them with your hair in worship.

- Anoint Him with the prayers of your praise for what He has done for you. Even if your sin was a long time ago, remember from where He has brought you and praise His name.

- If you are one of those who have never been found far from the Master, pray for those of us who have been.

- Thank God that everything He owns has belonged to you all along.

Forgiveness: The Freedom of Our Prayers

Forgiveness

1 John 1:9 (NKJV)
⁹If we confess our sins, He is faithful and just to forgive us *our* sins and to cleanse us from all unrighteousness.

Several years ago, I was talking with a friend on the phone; both of us are counselors. Given the "good" counselors that we were, we were in a conversation about people forgiving themselves. We were talking about how people caught in sin may have asked God to forgive them, maybe even asked others to forgive them, yet spend years punishing themselves for their sin.

We were discussing the benefits of forgiving oneself, when suddenly, a revelation came, and I started laughing. I saw the foolishness of people trying to forgive themselves. Only God has the right and the ability to forgive our sin. It is not a matter of forgiving self; it is a matter of receiving the forgiveness God already has for us.

Yes, we want to establish the need to forgive another person, to send the obligation away from us. Yes, it is important to seek forgiveness from others and allow God to restore broken relationships. And yes, it is very important that we "feel" the restoration of our broken fellowship with the Father after we have sinned. But we need not have any leftover shame or guilt in any of those areas.

The word for confess used in 1 John is "homologeo." To confess basically means to agree with God, we say the same thing He is saying about our sins. He is faithful, trustworthy, and worthy to be believed; what He says about sin is absolutely true. He is able to pinpoint the tiniest root of sin in our lives. The reason He wants it removed is because He knows the damage it will cause in your life—the one He loves so much. After we accept the fact of our sin and agree with God, we are ready to receive His forgiveness.

Only God is able to send away or dismiss our sins. Only He is able to remove our sins from us. To forgive sins is not to disregard them and do nothing about them but to liberate a person from them, their guilt, and their power. He sets us free based on what He accomplished at Calvary. That is something we can shout about from now through eternity.

> **Revelation 12:10 (NKJV)**
>
> [10]Then I heard a loud voice saying in heaven, "Now salvation, and strength, and the kingdom of our God, and the power of His Christ have come, for the accuser of our brethren, who accuses them before our God day and night, has been cast down."

> **John 8:44 (NKJV)**
>
> [44]You are of *your* father the devil, and the desires of you father you want to do. He was a murderer from the beginning, and does not stand in the truth, because there is no truth in him. When he speaks a lie, he speaks from his own *resources,* for he is a liar and the father of it.

> **1 John 5:17 (NKJV)**
>
> [17]All unrighteousness is sin, and there is sin not *leading* to death.

Why do we suffer so under the load of guilt if we have been liberated from our sins and from their power? We have an accuser who accuses us before God day and night. All lies come from the Devil. Our enemy would tell us that we have to pay for our sins, that Jesus Christ's payment was not enough. Satan would have us believe that God does not love us enough to forgive us. He exalts our sin to the place where we think it is too big for God to forgive. We act like the blood of Jesus is not enough payment, and we must help Him out by punishing ourselves. We think we have to feel bad over our sin even after we have asked God to forgive us.

When I have seen clients who were living under a load of self- and Satan-imposed guilt, I have often asked them, "How much punishment will be enough to pay for what you have done? How will you know when you have paid the full price?" Of course, nobody can tell me when he or she has suffered enough.

His promise is that He will cleanse us. He will purify us from the pollution and guilt of sin. He will cleanse us from anything that misses God's goal for us. If we are not submitted to His will and His goal for our lives, we are walking in unrighteousness. The seventeenth verse of 1 John 5 says that all unrighteousness is sin. If we are not submitted to God's will, we are submitted to Satan's will for our lives. Oh yes, Satan does have a will for us. Read 2 Timothy 2:26 in your Bible.

The key to being rid of the shame and guilt of our own sins is not to forgive ourselves but to accept the forgiveness of our God. I know it is difficult to accept that He really is that good. It is hard to comprehend that our sin debt has been paid in full—it all sounds too good to be true. When we refuse to accept fully the forgiveness offered to us and decide to impose punishment for our crimes, we are setting ourselves up as our own god.

Humble yourself before Him today as you pray. Bow before His presence and acknowledge His right to your life.

- Thank God for 1 John 1:9 and what it says.

- Read each word, thanking Him each step of the way.

- Agree with God about your sin and your sin nature.

- Confess anything the Holy Spirit brings to your mind.

Micah 7:19 (NKJV)
¹⁹He will again have compassion on us, and will subdue our iniquities. You will cast all our sins into the depths of the sea.

Psalms 103:12 (NKJV)
¹²As far as the east is from the west, *so* far has He removed our transgressions from us.

- Thank God that He casts all our sins into depths of the sea.

- Thank Him that He has removed our transgressions as far as the east is from the west. Praise God for those two things! He sends your sin away from you! Praise His name!

- If you have carried the weight of your sin after you have asked God to forgive it, confess that as sin.

- Confess that you have tried to be your own god and punish your sins. Confess you have tried to be your own Holy Spirit.

- Thank God that His mercy is new every morning. It is through His mercy that we are not consumed.

- Sit quietly for a while and meditate on the goodness of God. Think about His great mercies toward you. Let your heart turn toward Him in gratitude for His forgiveness toward you.

- Ask the Lord to help you receive and accept the fact that His forgiveness is for real. Yes, you mess up, but God _____. You fill in the blank. Hallelujah! Just reflect on His goodness until you feel it within.

Forgiveness: The Freedom of Our Prayers

Forgiveness and Prayer

Nehemiah 9:17 (NKJV)

[17]They refused to obey, and they were not mindful of Your wonders that You did among them. But they hardened their necks, and in their rebellion they appointed a leader to return to their bondage. But You *are* God, ready to pardon, gracious and merciful, slow to anger, abundant in kindness, and did not forsake them.

Psalms 130:4 (NKJV)

[4]But *there is* forgiveness with You, that You may be feared.

Luke 15:11–32 (NKJV)

[11]Then He said: "A certain man had two sons. [12]And the younger of them said to *his* father, 'Father, give me the portion of goods that falls *to me.*' So he divided to them *his* livelihood. [13]And not many days after, the younger son gathered all together, journeyed to a far country, and there wasted his possessions with prodigal living. [14]But when he had spent all, there arose a severe famine in that land, and he began to be in want. [15]Then he went and joined himself to a citizen of that country, and he sent him into his fields to feed swine. [16]And he would gladly have filled his stomach with the pods that the swine ate, and no one gave him *anything*. [17]But when he came to himself, he said, 'How many of my father's hired servants have bread enough and to spare, and I perish with hunger! [18]I will arise and go to my father, and will say to him, "Father, I have sinned against heaven and before you, [19]and I am no longer worthy to be called your son. Make me like one of your hired servants."' [20]And he arose and

came to his father. But when he was still a great way off, his father saw him and had compassion, and ran and fell on his neck and kissed him. ²¹And the son said to him, 'Father, I have sinned against heaven and in your sight, and am no longer worthy to be called your son.' ²²But the father said to his servants, 'Bring out the best robe and put *it* on him, and put a ring on his hand and sandals on *his* feet. ²³And bring the fatted calf here and kill *it,* and let us eat and be merry; ²⁴for this my son was dead and is alive again; he was lost and is found.' And they began to be merry. ²⁵Now his older son was in the field, and as he came and drew near to the house, he heard music and dancing. ²⁶So he called one of the servants and asked what these things meant. ²⁷And he said to him, 'Your brother has come, and because he has received him safe and sound, your father has killed the fatted calf.' ²⁸But he was angry and would not go in. Therefore his father came out and pleaded with him. ²⁹So he answered and said to *his* father, 'Lo, these many years I have been serving you; I never transgressed your commandment at any time; and yet you never gave me a young goat, that I might make merry with my friends. ³⁰But as soon as this son of yours came, who has devoured your livelihood with harlots, you killed the fatted calf for him.' ³¹And he said to him, 'Son, you are always with me, and all that I have is yours. ³²It was right that we should make merry and be glad, for your brother was dead and is alive again, and was lost and is found.'"

A few years ago, a person I loved dearly began calling me names and saying things I could not imagine anyone saying to another human being—especially to a person they supposedly cared about. I was cursed and screamed at many times over. I have no words to express the depth of my hurt and disappointment. I was treated in ways I could not conceive at the time. I was devastated to the core.

I remember when I first met this person. We were talking in my home when the Spirit of God within me spoke the words, "unconditional love." In my limited interpretation of God's Words, I thought, *Oh, she needs to experience unconditional love, and God is going to use me to do that.* I never thought that for me to love her unconditionally I would be hurt in the process. And I would never have considered how God could teach me about His unconditional love through the situation.

After the hurt occurred, I still loved the person as much as before. What God did was not what I had expected at all. Yes, I loved unconditionally, but I don't know that it had any affect except when I would tell this person that I loved her, she would sometimes cry and say, "I do not know why." Even in the middle of crying, the hurtful words and actions continued.

The thing that God did in all the hurt was to teach me what it means for Him to love me unconditionally. For years, I would express disbelief at how or why God would love me. During my hurt, I got the answer. I could no more stop loving my friend than I could turn myself into a frog. No matter how many times I was hurt, or how often, no matter how severe the pain, I just loved. Somewhere in the process, God revealed to me that I loved because of who I am, not because of the other person or what the other person does or does not do.

God showed me He loves me because of who He is, not because of who I am. His love does not change because of what I do or because of what I do not do. That is almost more than I can accept. That puts a stop to thinking I must be perfect for God to love me. Just like me with my friend, God could not help but love me; that is who He is. It is all about Him, nothing about me.

I could have tried to return the hurt for hurt. I could have destroyed a lot of things in my friend's life. It was within my power to do so, but it was not within my nature to do so. The same is true about God. He has the power to destroy any of us for any reason, but it is not within His nature to destroy His children. It is within His nature to love us and forgive us.

You might be wondering what all this has to do with forgiveness and prayer. Again, forgiveness gives freedom to our prayers. When we forgive, we are free to pray for those who despitefully use us. We are free to bless those who curse us. Just as love is within God's nature, so is forgiveness.

He is a God of forgiveness. Read the story of the prodigal son again. As you read the story this time, think about the fact that the father never once mentioned the son's sin. The focus of the father was on the relationship. He wanted it restored; he focused on the person.

It amazes me that the father never once mentioned what the son had done. He just loved him; he simply forgave him.

As you pray today:

- Thank God that He is a God of forgiveness. It is within His nature. He can do nothing else but forgive. Thank Him for His forgiveness in your life, whatever the measure.

- Thank God that His love is unconditional. He can do nothing but love you; it is within His nature.

- Thank God that because of His mercy we are not consumed. It is not within His heart to destroy His children.

- Thank God He forgives and does not bring it up to us ever again. Our sins are cast as far as the east is from the west.

- Thank God that He wants His relationship with you restored. Thank Him that His focus is not on your sin but on your relationship.

I believe these things are reasons to rejoice in His presence. Just begin to thank Him for all that is within you. Sing to Him! Praise Him out loud! He is worthy of all your praise!

CHAPTER 7

Communication: The Expression of Our Prayers

Matthew 6:5, 7 (NKJV)

[5]"And when you pray, you shall not be like the hypocrites. For they love to pray standing in the synagogues and on the corners of the streets, that they may be seen by men. Assuredly, I say to you, they have their reward. [7]And when you pray, do not use vain repetitions as the heathen *do*. For they think that they will be heard for their many words."

Psalms 37:4 (NKJV)

[4]Delight yourself also in the LORD, and He shall give you the desires of your heart.

Prayer is the expression of that which is within us to a God whom we believe can do something about the present situation. Prayer evolves from the desires of our heart. Prayer formed within us is based on our needs, hurts, losses, longings, grief, cares, concerns, and so on. It is made up of those things we wish for, we ask for, we want, and those things we believe would make life easier or better for ourselves or others. Something within us motivates us to look for God. Prayer should be communication between us and the Holy God.

According to a book called *The Power of Prayer in a Believer's Life*, compiled and edited by Robert Hall (Emerald Books, 1993), "True prayer is an approach of the soul by the Spirit of God to the Throne of God. It is not the utterance of words; it is not just the feeling of desires. It is the giving of our desires to God, the spiritual approach of our nature toward the Lord our God. True prayer is neither a mere mental exercise nor a vocal performance. It is far deeper than that. It is a spiritual transaction with the Creator of heaven and earth."

Expression is how we communicate to another that which is within us. An expression conveys meaning or a feeling. Different people have different methods of expression. It is impossible to not communicate to another. By trying to not communicate, we communicate our reluctance. Some people are more expressive than others.

Couples often come to me with a problem that they define as, "We do not communicate." While it is true that they may have poor or ineffective communication skills, trust me, everyone knows how to communicate their feelings. Withdrawal is communication, anger is communication, fear is communication, and silence is communication. There are all kinds of nonverbal ways of communicating through body language. The key for couples is to determine what they are trying to communicate and the methods they are using to convey the message. Hopefully, they can then learn to use effective, honest communication skills.

Let me ask you a question, do we always communicate something to God? When we are silent, does He get the message that He is not very important to us or that we are angry toward Him? What are we communicating when we say one thing to Him but feel another? Are we communicating that we really do not believe He knows our hearts? Are we saying we do not believe that He will accept us if we were totally honest with Him? If our prayers are the expression of our innermost being, what method do we use to express it?

Some people are quiet and calm when communicating. Others are dramatic, some even explosive. Some people talk with their hands. Some talk with their whole body. When you are very close to someone, you can communicate with just a look. Many times expressions of pain are seen on faces. Hugs are an expression of warmth and caring. Kisses, holding hands, laughing, and tears are all expressions.

In a normal church service, what expressions do we use to communicate something to our God? We think about the message. We sing praise to Him. We listen to the sermon. These are all forms of worship to our God.

What expressions of communication do you use in your private prayer time? What expressions of communication do you use in your worship time? What are we communicating to God and others when we sit in church with folded arms and silent week after week after week? What do we communicate to God and others by the expression on our face as we sit in worship service each week? What is it we are trying to express?

Just as interaction between two mortals takes various avenues, our communication with God is multifaceted. So far, we have discussed communication to God in terms of bowing before Him and either verbalizing our prayers or directing our thoughts toward God. Both ways are appropriate and useful, but I encourage you to practice verbalizing. Speaking seems to help keep us focused. Words stray less often than do our thoughts.

Effective communication requires you to say what you mean. Be sincere and honest. Some people beat around the bush when they talk. Why? They are afraid of not being accepted if they talk straight. They test the waters by getting close to the subject but not saying what they really want to say.

We often think God does not want to hear our true feelings. Are we afraid to express our true feelings to God? I think that we are. We are reluctant to tell God we are hurt, because He did not seem to come through for us. We are angry, because He could have changed something and He chose not to.

A lot of times we say what we think the other person will accept, and often, that is very different than what we really feel. When talking with humans, it is sometimes necessary to use sound judgment in what you say to another, but to God, it is not, He already knows anyway. In order to have an effective prayer life, we need to say what we really mean. In being free to be completely open and honest with God, we can have joy unspeakable and full of glory—because He loves us just the way we are. We are accepted and that is ample reason for great joy.

Honesty is the essence of our prayers. The essence of something is the fundamental nature of it. Essence is what makes it what it is. Honest, sincere words are the only substance of our prayers. Everything else is just words, floating around in the air.

In Matthew 6, Jesus is teaching that we should not pray to be heard. Isn't that exactly what we do most of the time? We pray what we think we are supposed to pray. We want it to sound good to other people's ears. I think we especially do that when we are in church. We say all the pretty church words that everyone else says. Most of the time, you can quote what someone is going to pray, especially if you have heard them pray before. I wonder if God is grieved by our insincere efforts.

How dare we use words intended to please the ears of those around us. We must realize that we are speaking to God Himself. We have business to transact with the King of Kings. Do we really think God is delighted to hear us use church words with a thoughtless mind? I think that some of our prayers are so prerecorded in our brain that we do not even have to think about them.

I get amused when I hear someone pray a dismissal prayer in church and ask God to bring us back at the next appointed time when they have no intention of coming back that night. They have no intention of coming back on Wednesday night, either. It is just something to say.

So, how are we to pray? We pray as we would talk to our Father if He were standing before us. We talk to Him about the things in our heart. I think the Scripture teaches us to come before His presence with thanksgiving and singing. We are to enter his gates with thanksgiving. We are to enter His courts with praise. It is always good to begin a prayer by thanking and praising Him. Somehow, that puts us in an attitude of receiving His presence. The Scripture teaches that God inhabits the praises of His people, so when you praise Him, He will show up.

When we are praying in public, I realize that you are praying somewhat of a different kind of prayer. You are offering up needs of many, not just your own. Even in doing that, you can be honest before Him. Sincerely pray what is in your heart, not just what sounds good to those around you.

Our prayers will not be as effective as they could be until we become transparent with the Father. It is acceptable to be angry at circumstances, to even tell God you are hurt at Him. It is okay to tell Him you do not understand why He did certain things. It is good to say things like, "I really do not feel like praying today, but I am going to because I know You have asked me to, and I know I need to." Just be careful to remember we are talking to God, and we are expected to maintain reverence for the fact that He alone is God and He is holy.

What I am trying to say is that we are to be totally honest with God about whatever you feel or think. Don't you think He might already know anyway? I do not believe that God is upset by our questions of Him. I do not think He is upset by our anger toward Him. We just need to discuss it with Him. We need to let Him show us the truth about the situation.

Would you be upset if your children misunderstood your actions and felt like you did not love them? As long as they did not tell you about their feelings, there would be a break in your fellowship. Once they told you about it, you could put your arms around them and tell them that you do love them and explain your behavior. We know God loves us and would not seek to hurt us. His ways are higher than ours, and we often misunderstand His actions. With that said, there are times when He does not explain His actions to us. He is not obligated to do so; if He does, it is because of His compassion. If He chooses not to tell us something, it may be that He is teaching us to trust Him.

There have been times I have been hurt at God, because I felt He could have done things differently on my behalf. I have been angry at some of my life's circumstances and told God so. I am not suggesting that we be disrespectful toward our gracious God. I am suggesting that we be honest and sincere.

Recently, a friend told me God had instructed her to quit her job and stay home. She quickly replied to Him by saying, "All right then, how are we going to take care of this bill and that bill, and besides, I do want to go to Alaska?" He quietly spoke to her and said, "Who do you think gave you Hawaii, and who do you think paid off your house?" He is wise enough to reply to our questions and emotions. My friend said that His words broke her heart. She quickly repented. So, a foundational element of an effective and joyful prayer life is being honest and sincere in the expression of our communication toward God.

We can express our communication to God in verbal and nonverbal ways. We can speak to Him. We can sing to Him. We can laugh with Him. We can shout to Him. We can also direct our thoughts toward God. We can raise our hands in praise or fold our hands in prayer. We can dance before Him. We can cry to Him. There are many ways that we can express our communication to God. These are just a few examples.

Psalms 30:4 (NKJV)

⁴Sing praise to the LORD, you saints of His, and give thanks at the remembrance of His holy name.

Psalms 47:6–7 (NKJV)

⁶Sing praises to God, sing praises! Sing praises to our King, sing praises! ⁷For God *is* the King of all the earth; sing praises with understanding.

Psalms 59:16 (NKJV)

¹⁶But I will sing of Your power; yes, I will sing aloud of Your mercy in the morning; for You have been my defense and refuge in the day of my trouble.

Proverbs 29:6 (NKJV)

⁶By transgression an evil man is snared, but the righteous sings and rejoices.

Isaiah 12:5–6 (NKJV)

⁵Sing to the LORD, for He has done excellent things; this *is* known in all the earth. ⁶Cry out and shout, O inhabitant of Zion, for great *is* the Holy One of Israel in your midst!

Psalms 32:11 (NKJV)

¹¹Be glad in the LORD and rejoice, you righteous; and shout for joy, all *you* upright in heart!

Psalms 35:27 (NKJV)

27Let them shout for joy and be glad, who favor my righteous cause; and let them say continually, let the LORD be magnified, who has pleasure in the prosperity of His servant.

Psalms 47:1–2 (NKJV)

1Oh, clap your hands, all you peoples! Shout to God with the voice of triumph! 2For the LORD Most High *is* awesome; *He is* a great King over all the earth.

Psalms 149:3–6 (NKJV)

3Let them praise His name with the dance; let them sing praises to Him with the timbrel and harp. 4For the LORD takes pleasure in His people; He will beautify the humble with salvation. 5Let the saints be joyful in glory; let them sing aloud on their beds. 6*Let* the high praises of God *be* in their mouth, and a two-edged sword in their hand.

Psalms 150:4, 5 (NKJV)

4Praise Him with the timbrel and dance; praise Him with stringed instruments and flutes! 5Praise Him with loud cymbals; praise Him with clashing cymbals!

Ecclesiastes 3:4 (NKJV)

4A time to weep, and a time to laugh; a time to mourn, and a time to dance.

Singing is a way of expressing thanksgiving, gratitude, praise, and worship. There are two different kinds of shouting. The first is when you become so full of joy or praise that it bubbles up within you. I suppose that you could stop it, but I think that it would be grieving to the Holy Spirit if you did. The second is a choice that you make to proclaim praise to Him. You may shout for joy or happiness. You cannot produce the first but you can the second. Shouting is a way of expressing joy, proclaiming His goodness, power, and triumph.

You don't really think that God gave us rhythm so that we could dance to country music or rock music, do you? We are created in His image.

Do you think that He dances? We have rhythm so that we can praise Him. Sometimes, when the presence of God is heavy, a congregation will start swaying without even realizing it. Whatever we do, we should do all for His glory. I have seen interpretive dance done in church, and it was beautiful. I have also seen people try to dance when it was obviously out of the flesh. It is all in the attitude of the heart. It is okay to dance before the Lord. It is okay to use rhythm in worship.

There are several ways that we use our hands to express what we feel toward God. We clasp or fold our hands in front of us as we pray. This is a symbol of hope and trust. It helps to direct our thoughts toward God in prayer. There have been times that I have wanted to stand and give God praise by clapping my hands. Many times in church, something said or done has caused me to want to stand to my feet and applaud His goodness.

You may notice that at different times you may extend your hands in different ways to the Lord. You may raise one or both hands with palms extended toward heaven. This is usually done when you are worshipping. You are giving to Him, praising Him, which is also an expression of trust, surrendering self. At other times, you may hold your hands close to your body, bent at the elbow, with palms upward, as if you are holding something. I believe at those times we are in a place of receiving something from God. All of these are expressions of worship.

How does God express His communication toward us? He did it in providing the supreme sacrifice in Jesus. That was the greatest expression of His love toward us. He fills us with the Spirit, at salvation and daily, as we allow Him to. He speaks to us through:

- His presence

- His Word

- Circumstances

- Other believers

- The goodness of God

- A restless spirit

- Unanswered prayers

Sometimes God speaks with more clarity than your family members. Other times He speaks in some of these other ways. I do not understand the difference. I am assured that His ways are higher than my own. He is trying to grow me up not just keep things from me. He is so gracious that He sometimes fills us so full of the Holy Spirit that we cry, we shout, we sing in praise and worship to His name.

Sometimes we hear at His feet. Other times we have to have pain before we hear Him. Why? I do not think it is His desire to give us pain. We sometimes will not receive His Word any other way. Pain of various kinds also produces maturity as the first chapter of James teaches. Pain is not a bad thing; it points out that something is wrong. Pain can also teach us about participating in the fellowship of His sufferings (Philippians 3:10).

Communication is, after all, between two parties. We need to wait to hear God before we leave our prayer time. We must meditate on His Word in His presence. We must expect to hear His voice. Consider the ways He might speak to you today. Remember He is the Creator—He can speak in ways you have never dreamed. If you have invited Him into your life and into your day, you can expect the divine. Ask Him to open your eyes and ears to see and hear today.

COMMUNICATION: THE EXPRESSION OF OUR PRAYERS

Devotionals

Communication: The Expression of Our Prayers

Singing: An Expression of Worship

Psalms 13:6 (NKJV)

⁶I will sing to the LORD, because He has dealt bountifully with me.

Psalms 21:13 (NKJV)

¹³Be exalted, O LORD, in Your own strength! We will sing and praise Your power.

Revelation 15:3–4 (NKJV)

³They sing the song of Moses, the servant of God, and the song of the Lamb, saying: "Great and marvelous *are* Your works, Lord God Almighty! ⁴Who shall not fear You, O Lord, and glorify Your name? For *You* alone *are* holy. For all nations shall come and worship before You, for Your judgments have been manifested."

Please understand that honesty in what you say or do in your prayer time is the essence of your prayer. There are many ways to express our feelings toward God. Today, we will be looking at singing as an expression of our worship toward God.

There are two aspects of singing that I want to bring out. Keep in mind that the expression of communication is a two-way street. We too often forget that God wants to express His love toward us as well as receive love from us. I believe that singing is a very important part of worship. I am also aware that we can sing without the engagement of our heart, and it is just pretty-sounding words, nothing else.

I know from personal experience that I can sing in the choir on Sunday morning or evening and never become engaged in expressing anything toward God. Then there are other times that I sing either in church or at home and something is different. I am directing the words and feelings toward God. That is when it becomes an expression of love toward my Father.

You might be thinking, *I know all of that already, it's simple stuff.* Yes, it is simple stuff, but if it is so simple, why do we not sing every time with that special expression of worship? I sit up front in my church in the choir loft and as I stand and sing, I can see the faces of those in the congregation. I know that the majority of the time most people are just like me. They are singing the words to the songs without the expression of feeling. It may be a simple concept, but it is a difficult concept to master.

God has given us this avenue of expressing attitudes, thoughts, and feelings toward Him. Scripture repeatedly encourages and commands us to "Sing unto the Lord." Singing is a God-given, God-blessed way of expression to our God and Father. Let us use it joyfully. God did not give you the ability to sing so that you might exalt Satan and his ways through the world's music. He gave it to us that we might worship Him.

Several years ago, while listening to praise music, God showed me how He was pleased that music was being played to praise Him. Words were being sung that exalted Him. Words that told of the great things He had done. Words that gave Him glory and honor. At the same time, He showed me how having the world's music only exalts Satan.

Why do you think Satan tries so hard to push the world's music? Because it is his music; it really is. I have read some the rock lyrics of songs out there. They never use Satan's name in vain. They never degrade Satan's name or his followers. Have you ever heard anyone say "Satan damn"? No, it is always God's name that is defamed. It is always God and Christians who get slammed. Have you ever stopped to wonder why?

I challenge you to test yourself sometime. How does listening to rock or country music make you feel? Does it put you in a mood to worship God? Does it put you in a mood to be reverent toward Him? Does it give you peace? Does it produce sensual feelings that get you in the mood to receive lustful thoughts? Does it make you agitated or rebellious? We must be guards of our own hearts.

I am not saying that there has never been a song other than gospel that was worth listening to. I am saying that we need to be extremely careful. I have been walking through a grocery store when some song would remind me of another time and place in my life. I have found myself getting depressed over a song that triggered a memory. On the whole, I believe that gospel music is much safer and more pleasing to the Father. You make your own choice.

Today in your prayer time:

- Listen to some good praise music. Let it get you in the mood to worship. Listen to the words.

- Ask God to make them real to you. Join in singing the songs. You may even want to sing one of your own to the Lord. This is His way of expression from you to Him. It was His idea.

Zephaniah 3:14–17 (NKJV)

¹⁴Sing, O daughter of Zion! Shout, O Israel! Be glad and rejoice will all *your* heart, O daughter of Jerusalem! ¹⁵The LORD has taken away your judgments, He has cast out your enemy. The King of Israel, the LORD, *is* in your midst; you shall see disaster no more. ¹⁶In that day it shall be said to Jerusalem: "Do not fear; Zion, let not your hands be weak. ¹⁷The LORD your God in your midst, the Mighty One, will save; He will rejoice over you with gladness, He will quiet *you* with His love, He will rejoice over you with singing."

- Please read the passage of Scripture from Zephaniah again. He will rejoice over you with gladness. He will quiet you with His love. He will rejoice over you with singing. Imagine, God singing over you! I told you that singing was His idea of expression.

- Ask the Lord to let you hear Him sing over you.

- Sit quietly before the Lord after you have sung to Him. Sit quietly before Him after you have listened to praise music. Sit before Him and meditate on the above Scripture. Imagine Him singing over you, because He is rejoicing over you, His beloved child. Is He good or what? After you have loved on Him, let Him love on you. Be blessed!

Before you are finished for today, read the Scriptures listed at the beginning of today's devotional.

- Praise God for the things mentioned in those Scriptures.

- Praise Him for His power.

- Praise Him for His bounty.

Communication: The Expression of Our Prayers

Lifting Your Hands in Praise

2 Chronicles 20:19–21 (NKJV)

[19]Then the Levites of the children of the Kohathites and of the children of the Kohahites stood up to praise the LORD God of Israel with voices loud and high. [20]So they rose early in the morning and went out into the Wilderness of Tekoa; and as they went out, Jehoshaphat stood and said, "Hear me, O Judah and you inhabitants of Jerusalem: Believe in the LORD your God, and you shall be established; believe His prophets, and you shall prosper." [21]And when he had consulted with the people, he appointed those who should sing to the LORD, and who should praise the beauty of holiness, as they went out before the army and were saying: "Praise the LORD, for His mercy *endures* forever."

Psalms 63:4 (NKJV)

[4]Thus I will bless You while I live; I will lift up my hands in Your name.

Psalms 134:2 (NKJV)

[2]Lift up your hands *in* the sanctuary, and bless the LORD.

Psalms 141:2 (NKJV)

[2]Let my prayer be set before You *as* incense, the lifting up of my hands *as* the evening sacrifice.

1 Timothy 2:8 (NKJV)

[8]I desire therefore that the men pray everywhere, lifting up holy hands, without wrath and doubting.

The way of expression of worship to God that we will look at today is lifting our hands. I realize that some of you may not be accustomed to raising your hands in worship. My purpose is not to make anyone uncomfortable. My purpose is to introduce the concept to you from a scriptural perspective. Look at it this way: if you do raise your hands in your prayer time, nobody will ever know it except for the Lord, and He just might smile on you!

According to well-known singer and songwriter Kent Henry, the above Scriptures are a reference for the word *Yadah*. Yadah is a word for praise meaning the extended hand, to throw out the hand, therefore to worship with extended hand. When I looked up "hands" in these Scriptures, I did find that the "hand" was often talking about the entire arm up to the shoulder. I also found reference to the palm of the hand being extended. All of these things together paint a picture of a person reaching upward, hands and arms extended with palms turned toward heaven.

I don't know if you have ever noticed it, but when people are filled with God's presence, they begin to testify or whatever, their hands just naturally raise toward heaven. When the Lord begins to fill me, I often have the urge to raise my hands to exalt Him. In my experience, when my hands are extended with palms toward heaven, I am giving worship to Him. I am feeling the urge to exalt and praise Him.

According to Henry, a second word for praise is *Towdah*. It is closely related to Yadah, except that it is more specific. It literally means an extension of the hand in adoration or acceptance. It is used for thanking God for things not yet received as well as things already received. Any way you look at it, the Scriptures teach us to use the instruments that God has given us to praise Him.

As you think logically of this position, it brings to mind a position of surrender, Surrender to God's will, surrender of yourself, of your will, of your ways, and so on. I picture a baby walking up to a parent and raising her hands to be picked up. That is a picture of trust, of dependence, of love.

Sometimes in God's presence, I find myself with my hands turned upward, my arms held close to my body. It is almost as if I am holding something. It is at those times that I am aware of receiving from the

Lord. Remember, communication is a two-way street. I may not understand what He is giving me, but it sure is sweet.

Today in your pray time, I want you to try something.

- Enter His gates with thanksgiving and His courts with praise.

- Once you are there, stand to your feet, lift your hands as high as you can, and begin to praise Him. Say aloud, "Lord, I thank You. I praise Your name. I bless You, Lord. Lord, You are Wonderful Counselor, Prince of Peace, Mighty God, Everlasting Father." Tell Him how you feel about Him, but do it with your hands raised toward Him. Give to Him the glory and honor He desires. If you prefer, use a psalm to tell Him how wonderful He is—just pray it back to Him.

Either today or tomorrow, in your prayer time:

- Ask God to reveal Himself to you in a clearer way.

- Kneel or sit before Him in quietness, with your hands extended in a way to symbolize receiving from Him.

- Ask Him to fill you with His Spirit. Sit and receive His infilling of His Spirit. He is so good. Taste and see that He is sweet!

Love and blessings!

Communication: The Expression of Our Prayers

Shout to the Lord

Today you have two options.

- After you have gotten to the place where you are experiencing God's presence, do as I suggested yesterday about extending your hands in receiving from God.

- Think about how much trust it requires to close your eyes and receive whatever He chooses to give you. Maybe this is a good time to get to the place where you are willing to receive the good, the bad, and the ugly.

What I mean is to get in a spiritual position to accept His ways as good and right, even when we do not understand them, to trust His sovereignty enough to know that whatever He allows in our lives is to mature us. Not to say that everything is good, but as long as we are walking in righteousness and not in deliberate sin, His ways are for our good.

- Ask the Lord to help you remain in a position to receive from Him, to receive all the blessings that He wants to give you. Be in a position for discipline as needed to receive whatever you need to make you like Jesus.

Your second option is to learn what it means to shout to the Lord. Some of you may want to close this book right now. I do not believe that you will. I believe that you will do whatever you think appropriate for where you are in your spiritual walk. You will learn from this, trust me.

Psalms 47:1 (NKJV)

¹Oh, clap your hands, all you peoples! Shout to God with the voice of triumph!

Psalms 35:27 (NKJV)

²⁷Let them shout for joy and be glad, who favor my righteous cause; and let them say continually, "Let the LORD be magnified, Who has pleasure in the prosperity of His servant."

Psalms 5:11 (NKJV)

¹¹But let all those rejoice who put their trust in You; let them ever shout for joy, because You defend them. Let those also who love Your name be joyful in You.

Psalms 32:11 (NKJV)

¹¹Be glad in the LORD and rejoice, you righteous; and shout for joy, all *you* upright in heart!

The word "shout" is from the word *shabach*, meaning to address in a loud tone, to triumph, glory, and shout. When was the last time that you addressed something or someone in a loud tone? Maybe you were at a ball game or another sports event where your children were involved.

Again, God did not give us volume just so that we could scream for the local ball team. He gave us volume so that we could shout to the Lord. Try it, you might like it. I am quite sure that God would.

Today:

- Consider all of the things that we raise our voices about.

- Think about the ways that you could use your voice for God.

- List each of those ways.

- Ask God to help you be willing to use your voice for Him. Would you be willing to proclaim His praise in a loud tone? If you are really courageous, do it.

- Tell Him how good He is loudly. Oh, come on, just one time. I promise I will not tell anyone that you did! Seriously, why are we so reluctant to do it? He is worthy, so worthy! Love and blessings!

Luke 19:37–38 (NKJV)

[37]Then, as He was now drawing near the descent of the Mount of Olives, the whole multitude of the disciples began to rejoice and praise God with a loud voice for all the mighty works they had seen, [38]saying, " *'Blessed is the King who comes in the name of the LORD!'* Peace in heaven and glory in the highest!"

Listen to the song titled "Shout to the Lord." Go ahead, sing along—loudly.

Communication: The Expression of Our Prayers

Identifying God's Voice

John 10:4–5, 27 (NKJV)

⁴**And when he brings out his own sheep, he goes before them; and the sheep follow him, for they know his voice. ⁵Yet they will by no means follow a stranger, but will flee from him, for they do not know the voice of strangers. ²⁷My sheep hear My voice, and I know them, and they follow me.**

John 10:16 (NKJV)

¹⁶**And other sheep I have which are not of this fold; them also I must bring, and they will hear My voice; and there will be one flock *and* one shepherd.**

Psalms 119:11 (NKJV)

¹¹**Your word I have hidden in my heart that I might not sin against You.**

I'm not sure about you, but sometimes I am not so sure that I know His voice. I have to believe it because the Scripture teaches it. I am insecure about knowing that it was His voice and not my own. I suspect that you are the same way. Much of what we will be studying today I have learned from Charles Stanley over the years. It is biblical and logical steps to being able to hear God's voice.

It is a normal experience to hear God's voice. We think it is unusual when we hear His voice, but it should not be so. God wants us to hear his voice and follow Him. His voice will be consistent with His Word. His Word will keep you from sin, not draw you into sin. If it is contrary to God's written Word, I can most assuredly say that it is not God's voice.

His voice is usually in conflict with human nature. He tells us to turn the other cheek. He tells us that His thoughts are not our thoughts. God will not tell us to gratify our flesh. If we forget what everyone else says and think, *I am going to do what I want to*, it is not God's voice that you hear. God's voice will not lead you to feed your flesh and disregard others.

God does not pressure you to make sudden moves. Satan encourages us to act immediately, often without prayerful consideration. He does not want us to have any time to pray or to think things through. He wants us to act rashly out of the desires of our flesh.

God's ways always consider the consequences. Satan says, "Eat, drink, and be merry, for tomorrow you may die!" We need to ask ourselves how this action or decision will affect our families. How will it affect my walk with God? Would I be ashamed to tell my grandchildren about my actions? We also need to seek Godly counsel. We need to seek the wisdom of Godly people we trust.

Sometimes we can go by a sense of peace. Use caution here, though. I have known people to have peace about committing suicide. Just remember that there is a false peace. The other things must also be in play. We have the ability to believe wrong is right.

God's direction will always produce spiritual growth. It will never set us back spiritually. God's voice will challenge our faith and, in doing so, will build our relationship with Him. We will grow in intimacy with Him. What He says in direction will oftentimes be something that we cannot do. It will challenge our faith. It will cause us to test our faith and trust of Him. Where He leads is not always easy.

You can also rest assured if what you hear is harsh or cruel, it is probably not God. God will never lead you anywhere your influence will be damaged. He wants your witness to be strong. When we walk in the Spirit, we have a Spiritual sensitivity to His voice. The problem is we do not always walk in the Spirit. Our ears are not turned to Him. We are too busy doing things our own way.

Today as you pray:

- Examine yourself to see how clearly you hear the Master's voice.

- Ask God to give you ears to hear Him only.

- Ask Him to help you go through this list of things before you make choices in the future.

- Ask God to make His voice clear to you.

- Be determined to wait until you hear Him before acting; commit that to God.

- Ask God to speak to you through His Word today. If you have a particular concern or request, ask Him to answer that prayer by showing you some truth in the Scripture. This means that you will have to meditate quietly on His Word while listening for Him to speak.

Communication: The Expression of Our Prayers

Increasing Our Ability to Hear Him

Jeremiah 33:3 (NKJV)

3"Call to Me, and I will answer you, and show you great and mighty things, which you do not know."

Psalms 46:10 (NKJV)

10Be still, and know that I *am* God; I will be exalted among the nations, I will be exalted in the earth!

1 John 5:14 (NKJV)

14Now this is the confidence that we have in Him, that if *we* ask anything according to His will, He hears us.

God sometimes uses things to get our attention when we fail to hear His voice. He may use words from others. He may use blessings. He may use unanswered prayers. He may use sickness. He may use a restless spirit to get our attention when we fail to hear His voice. Remember, hearing God should be a normal everyday experience for us.

There are practical things that we can do to increase our ability to hear Him. We should pray expecting to hear His voice. We should be quiet before Him. It is very important that we listen patiently for Him. After all, His timing is perfect. Not only should we listen patiently, we must listen confidently. Pray that God will reveal His will to you, that He will show you how to pray. Openly listen and be willing to obey. Carefully listen, sift everything through the Word of God.

When we pray, we must depend on the Holy Spirit to pray through us. He is the only One who knows what we really need. Be sure that you give God your full attention. Remember: be submissive, even if you do not like what you hear. Be grateful that God supplies all of our needs. Be very reverent toward God. We should be in awe that Holy God would speak to us and that He is listening to us.

When we fail to listen to God, we will listen to the wrong voices. We will also suffer the consequences of listening to the wrong voices. We can be easily deceived when we fail to listen to God. We will express pride and independence. By failing to listen to God, we will make decisions that appeal to the flesh. We will make excuses and blame others when we fail to listen to Him. When we fail to listen to God, it not only affects us, it affects others as well. We will cause others around us to suffer when we fail to listen to God, and we will miss out on God's best for us personally.

Today in your prayer time:

- Praise Him. Then, get yourself in an attitude of prayer.

- Ask God to make you sensitive to Him speaking through any or all of the ways we discussed in this chapter. Go back and list each way we discussed.

- Think about each one, and ask Him to reveal any time that He has tried to speak through these things.

- Ask God to help you do whatever is necessary to listen to His voice.

- Pray that God will keep you from hearing the wrong voices and experiencing any of those things we looked at in today's devotional. Look at each one separately, and ask God to deal with that issue within you.

Finally, I want you to get out some paper and a pen. Write out a question that you have for God, a prayer. Really expect Him to answer it. Write down what comes to your mind. Continue to do this as long as you want. Remember, all words should be sifted through the Word of God and all of the other principles we have looked at this week.

Be blessed!

CHAPTER 8

Peace: The Benefit of Our Prayers

We have discussed many foundational elements about prayer. My question to you now is, why pray? What benefit is there in prayer? Does God really hear our prayers? If He hears our prayers, does He care? If I pray, will He answer my prayer? Will God do what I ask of Him? If He does not do what I ask, then why should I pray?

Why did Paul pray to God? God could have removed the thorn of the flesh from Paul's life. After all, God Almighty is the One who is able to do what He wants. He could have removed the thorn. God is also able to remove your problem if He chooses. He could remove that thing or situation within you that you have struggled with all of your life. Or it could be a recent event that you struggle with. You may have prayed, believing that you were being sincere, and yet the situation still remains. God did not fix things for you. So why should you keep praying to God?

Isaiah 26:3 (NKJV)
³**You will keep** *him* **in perfect peace,** *whose* **mind** *is* **stayed** *on You,* **because he trusts in You.**

When we are anxious about a situation, we are not aligned with God. Do you suppose that God is anxious? Do you suppose that God is disrupted in personality or mind? Is He troubled about your situation? No, God is not anxious, nor is He disrupted in personality or mind.

Prayer then, according to this Scripture, reconciles us to oneness with God. It changes our perspective of things. Our focus leaves the problem and goes to the source. We can have peace. God wants us to have peace.

Prayer releases our concerns to Him and places them before Him, as if we are handing them to Him. By releasing our concerns to Him, it removes them from our shoulders. We no longer have to bear the burden alone! Prayer gives Him the responsibility for the outcome of the situation or problem.

Prayer reconciles us to Him. It aligns us to His will, not to our own will. It makes us one with Him again. Prayer reminds us that He is in control. He is not obligated to answer our prayers in the way we see and want; He sees the whole picture. He does according to His will for our lives. He does not act according to our momentary urges. He knows exactly what we need and when we need it.

When we become attuned to the Holy Spirit, our prayers begin to line up with His will. When we focus on Him, our heart will cease to be troubled. It allows us to build a relationship with the Father. Prayer allows us direct communication with God. Prayer places us in the throne room, where God awaits.

Prayer produces hope, surety, and confidence within us. It gives us hope about the situation because we know God Almighty. Prayer places us in a place of worship. Prayer produces peace and a quiet mind.

Philippians 4:6–7

6Be anxious for nothing, but in everything by prayer and supplication, with thanksgiving, let your requests be made known to God; 7and the peace of God, which surpasses all understanding, will guard your hearts and minds through Christ Jesus.

Do not let anything trouble you and bring disruption to your mind and personality. Pray to God, and let your specific need be known to

Him. Tell Him exactly what you need. Present your request or need in the midst of thanksgiving for His past mercies. Recognize that He has moved on your behalf before, and He is fully able to move now.

When you are able to do this, the peace of mind and tranquility that comes from being reconciled with God will fill and preserve your emotions, your desires, your impulses, and your intellectual understanding. This peace is superior to or more excellent than any understanding. Even if you cannot understand how God could do it, and you probably cannot, there is peace. This peace will come through resting in Jesus. It will come when you realize that He is Lord of everything and is able to do exceedingly abundantly above all that you might ask or think.

10 Results of Prayer (by Charles Stanley)

1. Personal testimony.
2. Perspective is enlarged.
3. Positive faith attitude.
4. Peace in the midst of pressure.
5. Purifying effect in your life.
6. Pathway to true spiritual growth in every area.
7. Passion to obey God.
8. Provision for every need.
9. Power in your service for God.
10. Productive in every area of life.

Philippians 4:8 (NKJV)

[8]Finally, brethren, whatever things are true, whatever things *are* noble, whatever things *are* just, whatever things *are* pure, whatever things *are* lovely, whatever things *are* of good report, if *there is* any virtue and if *there is* anything praiseworthy—meditate on these things.

PEACE: THE BENEFIT OF OUR PRAYERS

Devotionals

Peace: The Benefit of Our Prayers

My Mind Stayed on Him

Isaiah 26:3 (NKJV)
³**You will keep** *him* **in perfect peace,** *whose* **mind** *is* **stayed**
on You, **because he trusts in You.**

What exactly does it mean for you to have your mind stayed on Him? The Hebrew word for "stayed" in this passage means to lean upon or take hold of. There is nothing to take hold of or lean upon that is secure, except God. The word for "perfect peace" is the Hebrew word *shalom* and is described as a satisfied condition and an unconcerned state. Of course, peace has to do with the idea of rest and security (*The Complete Word Study Dictionary*).

Most of us find this a very difficult thing to accomplish. If it were impossible, God would not have mentioned it to us. We tend to pray about something and continue to carry it away with us. I really think that the bottom line is a spiritual issue of trust. In all honesty, we tend to trust our own efforts more than we trust this unseen God. Our lack of trust reflects our lack of intimacy with the Father.

How do we lean on or rest ourselves upon Him? Remember, we are talking about resting our minds. What would a steadfast mind be like? *Merriam Webster's Dictionary* defines "steadfast" as firm, fixed, or established, constant, not changing or fickle. Does that describe the way your mind works? Does that describe the way you handle your concerns—by leaning every concern onto the Lord and taking hold of His truth?

How often do we waver on what to do in a given situation? Wouldn't it make more sense and save a lot of time if we prayed about it and rested on the fact that our Father heard us and will do what He alone knows is best? Yes, it would. I think that we find it difficult to accept the fact that He really does love us, that he is good and does what is best for us. Again, it is a trust issue.

Examine your own heart. Do you trust God in a way that you feel safe, secure, and confident? For those of us who have been hurt in the past, those of us who have had the "rug pulled out from under us," it is more difficult to trust. Are you willing to trust this God, who gave so much to have a relationship with you?

Today as you pray, prepare your heart before Him.

- Ask the Lord to examine your heart and reveal issues that are preventing your complete trust.

- Ask him to reveal any past hurts that developed into resistance to trusting Him.

- Ask Him to help you keep your mind "stayed" upon Him.

- Ask Him to keep your mind steadfast and sure upon Him.

- Ask Him to help you trust that He will not pull the rug out from under you.

- Ask God to give you a glimpse of His goodness toward you, of His thoughts toward you.

Think about one specific situation you are concerned about. Present it to the Lord. Ask Him to allow you to see the situation from His perspective. Pray about it; give it to Him, pray until you have perfect peace about Him, not necessarily about the situation.

Praise His name! He is worthy of your trust!

Peace: The Benefit of Our Prayers

Where Peace Comes From

Isaiah 9:6 (NKJV)

⁶For unto us a Child is born, unto us a Son is given; and the government will be upon His shoulder. And His name will be called, Wonderful, Counselor, Mighty God, Everlasting Father, Prince of Peace.

Philippians 4:9 (NKJV)

⁹The things which you learned and received and heard and saw in me, these do, and the God of peace will be with you.

Ephesians 2:14–15 (NKJV)

¹⁴For He Himself is our peace, who has made both one, and has broken down the middle wall of separation, ¹⁵having abolished in His flesh the enmity, *that is*, the law of commandments *contained* in ordinances, so as to create in Himself one new man *from* the two, *thus* making peace.

Today we want to look at just where peace comes from. Jesus is called the Prince of Peace. The word "Prince" refers to the Head, the Master, the Ruler, and the Commander. He is the One who controls peace, thus He is called the God of Peace. Peace comes from a state brought about by the grace and loving mind of God, wherein the derangement and distress of life caused by sin is removed. This has to do with being reconciled to God. As I said earlier, to be at peace is to be aligned with God.

He Himself is our peace. All that He did He did to bring peace to earth. When the angels announced His birth, they said, "Glory to God in the highest, and on earth, peace, good will toward men." He is all about peace. He reconciles men to God and calms our anxiety by giving us a steadfast, untroubled mind. How can we have a mind like that? We can by understanding the sovereignty of God.

Matthew 10:29–31 (NKJV)

²⁹Are not two sparrows sold for a copper coin? And not one of them falls to the ground apart from your Father's will. ³⁰But the very hairs of your head are all numbered. ³¹Do not fear therefore; you are of more value than many sparrows.

The Scripture from Matthew 10 is one of the best Scriptures that describe God's Sovereignty in a nutshell. A sparrow cannot die of natural causes or be shot down by some child's BB gun without the Father's will. Do not miss that. It is not just that He is aware a sparrow dies. He must give permission for it to even happen. He goes on to say that He knows us so well that He knows the number of hairs on our head. He said, "Do not fear therefore." Since He knows us that well and everything that touches us must go through Him first, there is no need to be afraid—if we trust Him.

I realize that we often worry about the future. Can you imagine the peace we would have if we trusted that absolutely nothing was going to touch our lives unless it was the Father's will? That would also mean we trusted His love for us that He allowed only those things that would produce good in us and for us.

Today as you pray:

- Meditate on these scriptural principles.

- Ask God to help you grasp the truth of His Sovereignty. Ask God to deliver you from fear and to enable you to trust Him completely. What else can we do since we cannot make ourselves breathe another breath or cause our hearts to beat another time? He has shown Himself to be trustworthy so many times. How many of you can recall a time when God protected you or provided for you when you did not even realize your need? Some of you have had sickness in you body that God knew about long before you did. Trust Him; He is big enough to handle our problems, and *nothing* is beyond His reach.

- Thank and praise God that He is in absolute control of everything. Therefore, we can and should rest in Him.

Peace: The Benefit of Our Prayers

My Needs, God's Provisions

Matthew 6:8 (NKJV)

⁸"Therefore do not be like them. For your Father knows the things you have need of before you ask Him."

Luke 12:22–31 (NKJV)

²²Then He said to His disciples, "Therefore I say to you, do not worry about your life, what you will eat; nor about the body, what you will put on. ²³Life is more than food and the body *is more* than clothing. ²⁴Consider the ravens, for they neither sow nor reap, which have neither storehouse nor barn; and God feeds them. Of how much more value are you than the birds? ²⁵And which of you by worrying can add one cubit to his stature? ²⁶If you then are not able to do *the* least, why are you anxious for the rest? ²⁷Consider the lilies, how they grow: they neither toil nor spin; and yet I say to you, even Solomon in all his glory was not arrayed like one of these. ²⁸If then God so clothes the grass, which today is in the field and tomorrow is thrown into the oven, how much more *will He clothe you,* O *you* of little faith? ²⁹And do not seek what you should eat or what you should drink, nor have an anxious mind. ³⁰For all these things the nations of the world seek after, and your Father knows that you need these things. ³¹But seek the kingdom of God, and all these things shall be added to you."

Philippians 4:19 (NKJV)

¹⁹And my God shall supply all your need according to His riches in glory by Christ Jesus.

I do not know the needs and concerns of everyone who is reading this book, but I do know that we all have them. Some of us worry about health concerns. At times, most of us think about what we would do if we lost our spouse. Most of us have had financial concerns and at times worried about how to make ends meet. It is a different worry or concern for each of us, but we all have worries and concerns.

Have you ever noticed that there seems to be a direct relationship between the degree of concern and our degree of closeness with the Father? Maybe it is not so for you, but for me it is true. My perspective changes as I stand in His light. It is so amazing. His light casts a whole different light on the situation.

Fear is the opposite of faith. Faith is the substance of things hoped for, the evidence of things not seen. Fear is the substance of things *not* hoped for, the evidence of things we hope will never be seen. Fear is belief in and dwelling on the thought or possibility of something negative happening. It is dread of danger that may never occur. How much of our time and energy is stolen from us for this cause? Fear is faith in the lies placed before us by Satan. Faith is belief in the truth of God.

Read the Scripture from Matthew 6:8 and Luke 12:22–31 again. Read it again. As you read it for the second or third time, meditate on it and praise God for each promise to you through this Scripture. The passage in Philippians states that God will supply all of our needs according to His riches in glory by Christ Jesus. That sounds like a statement you can trust! (Of course, we must read all scripture in context) Thank God for opportunities to give to kingdom purposes. Thank Him that He will remember your generous giving. Praise God for His goodness!

In our country right now, many people are concerned about our economy. After the terrorist attacks of September 11, 2001, many people lost their lives, jobs, homes, and a sense of security. We are uncertain about safety issues. We really do not feel secure with our retirement. We even worry about the shortage of gasoline and food as well as electricity. In some ways, we have been shaken to the core.

I am by no means suggesting that these things could not happen to us. I am suggesting that we serve a God who already knows what we will face in the future. He is not shaken. He is not wondering about what to do. He already knows. He is in control.

Psalms 37:25 (NKJV)

²⁵I have been young, and *now* am old; yet I have not seen the righteous forsaken, nor his descendents begging bread.

- Thank Him that He will never forsake you.

- Thank Him that you are "the righteous," and you will never have to beg for bread.

- Please read Luke 12:22–31 again and glean all the security that you can from that passage of Scripture. Thank Him for each part.

- Praise Him for His provision.

- Thank Him that He knows your need even before you ask.

- Thank Him that before you are aware of the need, He is already sending you provisions.

- Thank Him for the security of our future in Him.

Peace: The Benefit of Our Prayer

Peace and Our Future

Psalms 122:6 (NKJV)

⁶Pray for the peace of Jerusalem: "May they prosper who love you."

Genesis 12:1–3 (NKJV)

¹Now the LORD had said to Abram: "Get out of your country, from your family and from your father's house, to a land that I will show you. ²I will make you a great nation; I will bless you and make our name great; and you shall be a blessing. ³I will bless those who bless you, and I will curse him who curses you; and in you all the families of the earth shall be blessed."

Today we are still going to focus on peace as related to our future. We all realize that our country is at war, maybe for years to come. We all know those who are or who may be or have been in dangerous places. Let us look at part of the reason these things must be.

As you know, part of the reason America was attacked on September 11, 2001, was because we as a country support the nation of Israel. Of course, that is only part of the reason. We are too liberal in our beliefs and behaviors in contrast to the beliefs of radical extremists, who have a distorted religious belief. The terrorists see our nation as following Satan. I cannot defend the things associated with our culture that do follow Satan. We must realize the seriousness of these recent threats to our own religious beliefs and freedoms. You can rest assured that if whoever orchestrated that whole mess were to have his way, our religious freedoms would come to a screeching halt.

Who knows? Our nation my go through some trimming away like the vinedresser does the vineyard. God is still in control, though. We must remember that we are His children, and He is responsible for our care. Praise His name; He is up for the challenge! We must remember, no matter what, we are His, and regardless of what happens, we are safe in His care. Where could you be any safer than in the hand of Almighty God? This does include your loved ones, wherever they may be.

God told Abraham that those who bless Israel would be blessed. He told him that those who cursed Israel would be cursed. As a country, the United States may get a lot of pressure from other nations because, as a nation, we do support Israel. Thank God that we do support Israel. I certainly do not want to have God curse our nation.

Today as you pray:

- Thank God again that He is in control of all circumstances.

- Thank Him that you are safe in His hand.

- Pray that the leaders of our country and other leaders would continue to have the wisdom to support Israel fully.

- Pray for the peace of Jerusalem.

- Pray for the prosperity of Jerusalem.

- Pray for other nations to understand the truth of supporting Israel.

- Pray for the peace of God to rule this earth. I am not so naïve to believe that there will ever be peace in the Middle East, not until Jesus returns, but I can pray for the God of Peace to rule the hearts of the people in those countries.

Nothing I have talked about in this devotional was said to cause you anxiety. I have said nothing that we all have not already thought about. Although, I do think it is urgent for us to pray for our leaders to continue to support Israel.

Peace: The Benefit of Our Prayers

The Holy Spirit and Peace

John 16:33 (NKJV)

³³"These things I have spoken to you, that in Me you may have peace. In the world you will have tribulations; but be of good cheer, I have overcome the world."

Please read the entire fourteenth chapter of the book of John.

The fourteenth chapter of John is a comforting passage to me. I know we have heard it used in a lot of funerals, but to me, it is encouraging. He comforts us right off the bat by saying, "Let not your heart be troubled; you believe in God, believe also in Me." He goes on to assure readers that He has made provisions for them.

I also believe that He is talking in intimate terms when He says that He goes to prepare a place for you. I believe it is a place, a dwelling place, designed especially for you. He knows your likes and dislikes. He is more aware than you of what makes you smile. He loves us so much I believe He prepares each place with painstaking loving care to express His love for us.

Later in the chapter, Jesus talks about leaving the Holy Spirit as our Helper. He will abide with us forever. That means that the Holy Spirit will live or dwell with us forever. Jesus talks about the Holy Spirit and peace. Is He saying that the Holy Spirit is our avenue of peace? The Holy Spirit knows the will of God and the mind of God. It is through the presence of the Holy Spirit that we receive the peace of God.

Be encouraged, dear friend, we have won. We are on the victorious side. Do not be afraid, or be dismayed; our God reigns!

Prepare your heart for time before Almighty God today. Rejoice before Him. Sing to Him. Acknowledge His authority over your life and submit to that authority. As you pray:

- Meditate on the above Scriptures.

- Thank God for the Helper, which is the Holy Spirit, who abides with you forever.

- Ask the Lord to help you make the Holy Spirit welcome in your life.

- Thank God for leaving His peace with us. Thank Him for peace that passes all understanding.

- Thank Him for the peace of reconciliation (salvation) as well as the ability to cast our cares upon Him.

- Thank Him for the resulting peace of knowing that He cares for us.

- Thank Him that He is able to do exceedingly and abundantly above all that we might ask or think, according to the power within us.

- Thank God that though we may have tribulation in this world, in Him we can have peace. Please do not just say these words, but ask the Lord to help you pray these things from your heart. Do not stop until things change, and you know you have been in His presence.

CHAPTER 9

Righteousness: The Strength of Our Prayers

What does righteousness have to do with prayer? Well, first of all as we learned in chapter 1, our prayers are not heard in the aspect of moving the hand of God unless we have Jesus as our Savior. When we receive Jesus into our heart, we are receiving all that He has to offer, including His righteousness.

> **Isaiah 61:10 (NKJV)**
>
> **I will greatly rejoice in the Lord, my soul shall be joyful in my God; for He has clothed me with the garments of salvation, He has covered me with the robe of righteousness, as a bridegroom decks himself with ornaments, and as a bride adorns herself with her jewels.**

> **Psalms 11:7 (NASB)**
>
> **For the Lord is righteous, He loves righteousness; the upright will behold His face.**

Within ourselves, we have no righteousness. Isaiah 64:6 declares that we are all like an unclean thing and our righteousness is as filthy rags. And we know that filthy rags refer to cloths used to cover leprous sores, which would be filled with infection. Not a positive picture of any righteousness on my behalf. Compared to the holiness of God, anything I could make myself do in the way of moral uprightness is still rottenness to the core. To try within ourselves to be good, more often than not, results in personal failure and disappointment.

How then can we be righteous? If we could be good enough to attain a righteous state, Jesus would not have had to die. Accepting that without Him and His robe of righteousness we are morally bankrupt is the first step to becoming righteous.

First, we come to Jesus in our unrighteousness and accept His righteousness. He places His robe of righteousness on us. I love to picture Jesus placing a robe of His righteousness on my shoulders. I can't help but wonder if it has been dipped in His blood and somehow comes out whiter than I can imagine, and when He places it on me, I also become whiter and purer than I can imagine with my human mind. I love to imagine the gentleness with which He places it on me. I love the warmth of the feeling it brings even in my imagination. Once He has placed His robe on me, I stand in His righteousness, not my own. Now, when the Father looks at me, He sees the righteousness of His Son instead of my failing efforts.

Because I know my faults, failures, and weaknesses, it is hard for me to imagine that God looks at me and sees the righteousness of Jesus. It is difficult in one way, yet easy in another way, to receive the unspeakable love of God with all its benefits. Maybe that is one reason Jesus said we must come as a little child. A child does not worry about their unworthiness but expects to receive and readily accepts love from a parent. If only adults could as easily as children receive what God wants to give.

Once we have the empowering presence of God within us, we are not only just relying on our human efforts when we pursue righteousness. We are then commanded and expected to be righteous. Anything He asks us to do He will also equip us to do. He is the Master, and we are His servants. He provides all necessary materials for building anything, including building a life. From that point forward, we are not alone in the reach for righteousness.

The above Scripture from Psalm 11 says that God is righteous and He loves righteousness. Have you ever wanted to know what God loves and deems important? I think this Scripture gives us a pretty good picture. He loves righteousness. He loves to see someone acting righteously. He loves righteous deeds.

The last part of that verse says the righteous will behold His face. Do you want to behold His face? Do you want to see Him? And I mean "see Him" in the sense of perceiving Him and His pleasure. Do you want to really know Him? Then align your life with His standards.

When we come to Jesus, we are given His righteousness, therefore, when God looks at us, He sees us as He would see Jesus: His righteousness is imparted to us. We are in a covenant relationship with Him. Our robe of unrighteousness has been exchanged for His robe of righteousness. It is a permanent covenant relationship. But if we want to have power and intimacy with God, we must go beyond that point. Many people are saved—meaning they have asked Jesus into their heart—but they have not become a follower of Jesus. A true follower or disciple of Jesus must embrace the Master's teaching and make it the basis for the conduct of their life. To be a disciple, a learner was taught to do everything the Teacher did, to talk like the Teacher, to act like the Teacher. A disciple believed that they were to do everything the Teacher did. That is why Peter decided to walk on the water; he knew if his Teacher did it, he was supposed to be able to also—and he did.

It is interesting to me that the meaning of righteousness is very similar to that of disciple. A disciple made the Master's teachings the basis for his conduct of life. A righteous man is one who aligns himself with the standards of God—his Master. In both cases, the person is acting like their Master. They are active in changing their lives to match that of the One they are following. They are disciplining themselves, that is, training themselves to walk by the Spirit and not by the flesh. They no longer allow their flesh to dictate their behavior; they no longer do everything and anything they want. Rather, they do what the Master says is right.

Let me clarify once again: we are not made righteous by our good works or aligning ourselves with the Master's teaching. We receive the righteousness of Jesus at salvation. But if you want to have power with God, you must act as He does, make His teachings the basis for your conduct. You must align your life with that of the standards of a Holy and Righteous God.

I am a visual learner. If I watch someone do something, I am much more likely to be able to imitate that behavior than if I just read about it in a book. Doesn't it just make sense that if Jesus had so much power and He lived under a certain standard, if we want the same, we might consider living by the same standard, that is, to imitate Him?

I know we have used this Scripture before, but we are going to use it again. Let's once again look at Isaiah 6:1–3. I do not know about you, but I don't have the power in prayer that I'd like to have. Sometimes you hear people pray and things happen immediately. I don't always see results that quickly. As a matter of fact, I have at times waited years to see the results of my prayers. I read about Elijah and Elisha and wondered how they had so much power in prayer and it seems that I did not.

James 5:16–17 describes the kind of prayer I am talking about. Beginning in verse 16 it says, "Therefore confess your sins one to another and pray for one another [the *King James Version* says confess your faults] that you may be healed. The effective prayer of a righteous man can accomplish much. Elijah was a man with a nature like ours and he prayed earnestly that it might not rain and it did not rain on the earth for three years and six months, and he prayed again and the sky poured rain and the earth produced its fruit" (NASB).

Now that is the kind of prayer life I would like to have. I know you probably think, *Yeah, but that was Elijah.* Do not miss the part of the verse that says that Elijah had a nature like ours, which is basically saying he was just like you and me. I want to know how Elijah can pray with such dramatic results and I can't. Maybe you do. Maybe you can pray that it does not rain for three years, and it doesn't. Then you pray again, and it does rain. I will be honest with you: I have not seen any of us praying that way lately. Why can Elijah pray with such effectiveness and we cannot, or don't. Some say it is faith, but I am not convinced that faith is the entire answer.

In thinking about this subject, I want to discuss one thing I found that relates to the strength or effectiveness of prayer: our righteousness. We will talk more about what righteousness is in a minute, but first, let's go back to the Isaiah 6 passage, because I want you to notice something there. In verse 5, it says, "So I said, woe is me for I am undone for I am a man of unclean lips and I dwell in the midst of a land of people of unclean lips. For my eyes have seen the king the Lord of Hosts, then one of the Seraphim flew to me, having in his hand a live coal which he had taken from the altar with tongs. And he touched my mouth with it and said, 'Behold, this has touched your lips; and your iniquity is taken away and your sin forgiven.' Then I heard the voice of the Lord saying, 'Whom shall I send, and who will go for us?' Then said I, Here am I. Send me."

The first part of this Scripture describes Isaiah seeing the holiness of God; he saw the Lord high and lifted up. Please pay close attention to the fact that it was only *after* Isaiah realized the holiness of God that he was able to say, "Woe is me, for I am a man of unclean lips." Consider this; Isaiah had to see the holiness of God before he could see his own sin. When you look at God, there is something like a mirror that opens up within our spirits and minds. When you are in God's presence and you see God, somehow there is a reflective element involved, and you see yourself in a different light. When Isaiah looked at the Lord and saw the Lord's holiness, then and only then was he able to see himself. When Isaiah said, "For my eyes have seen the King the Lord of Hosts," he was saying because, or by reason of. He was saying I see my unrighteousness *because* I have seen the righteousness and holiness of the Lord.

In 1 John 3:2, it says that we shall be like Him, for we shall see Him as He is. I believe that verse is saying the more we see Him and the more we view Him, the more we will become like Him. Do you know that if you dwell on something long enough, you will become like that something, which becomes your focus? For example, if you determine you will not be like your mother or father but you continue to keep that person in your mind's view, you will become like them. You may be determined to be the opposite, but the more you focus on them, the more you become conformed to their image because they are all that is in your view. So then, we must keep God in our vision.

When we come to the place where we see Him as He is, we will be like Him. The more we are in His presence, the more we see Him high and lifted up. The more like Him we will then become, because then and only then, we will see ourselves in truth. When we look at Him, there is a reflective nature, and we see ourselves in truth, which causes us, as Isaiah, to say, "Woe is me for I am undone and I am a person of unclean lips and I live in a land of people of unclean lips." So, Lord, please move in my life. It was only after he saw God that he was able to see himself as he really was.

Scripture says in Isaiah 6 that one of the seraphim flew, having in his hand a live coal, and so on and so forth; you know the Scripture. Only after Isaiah recognized his sinful condition was the Lord able to move. Have you ever noticed that about yourselves or church services? As long as you're in this little—for lack of a better word—prideful attitude of me, myself, and I, all the while refusing to really look at yourself, God doesn't move in your life. He doesn't seem to be very impressed with our prideful attitude. You have to come to a place where you acknowledge where you are and then God moves in you to clean you up. Not before. As long as you do not acknowledge your need, He does not come and clean you up. It is like you cannot be saved until you get lost.

Isaiah saw how rotten he was. I personally believe he was saying, "I have a problem with my mouth." I think this was pretty literal; he was confessing that he had some kind of issue with what proceeded from his heart through his mouth.

The word "seraphim" there comes from the verb seraph, and it literally means to burn. So again, I think this is all very literal. The seraph took the coal off the altar and put it on the lips of Isaiah and said, "Your sin is taken away." In some translations, then is used again in verse 8—then I heard the voice saying. First, he had to see God before he could then see himself. Second, his situation had to be cleaned up before he heard the voice of the Lord. So, from this one verse of Scripture, you can see how unrighteousness comes into play with you hearing the Word of God.

The word "holiness" in the Greek carries with it the idea of separation, separation from sin and from that which contaminates. That is a theme in this lesson. Holiness is being free from that which contaminates. And holiness is moral purity in the midst of that which is unholy and profane. The words "saint" and "sanctified," which has been used to describe the child of God, has the same root word as the word "holy." Saint—holy. So, we understand true holiness when we see God as He really is.

When I was looking up the definition of confess, I found something I had not noticed before. We have said that to confess is to agree with God, and it is. But another part of the definition is to externalize that which is on the inside of oneself. James says to confess your faults one to another. I think what that is saying is that I am to vomit what is on the inside of me to a Christian brother or sister. I think it is saying that what is on the inside of me and what is on the outside of me should agree. Just like confess is to agree with God. If I confess my sin, I say to God, "You're right, this is sin, this is wrong, it should not be." To confess my fault one to another is to bring out what is on the inside of me. So, I would say to you, "I don't really want to admit this, but here is the fault that is within me—rottenness in some form." To confess a trespass one to another is an expression of being human. Trespass is to fall by the wayside, error, or mistake: it is the exact opposite of righteousness. Of course, we know what pray means: confess your faults one to another, pray for one another, and you will be healed. Healed metaphorically means of moral diseases, or to heal or to save from the consequences of sin or to bring safely through. To be healed can be to be brought to bodily health, but metaphorically, it is to be healed of moral diseases or saved from the consequences of sin (*The Complete Word Study Dictionary*). Confess your faults one to another, and pray for one another that you may be healed. Could it be that God is saying that as the body of Christ we should externalize that which is on the inside of us to our brothers and sisters? We should be able to and then willing to pray for one another. When they confess or when we confess, the atmosphere should be one of safety and confidentiality. The resulting healing could be literal physical healing, but it could also be saving from the consequences of the sin.

The effectual or effective fervent prayer of a righteous man avails much. An effectual prayer is one that produces an effect. That makes sense, doesn't it? It puts forth power, it is active, it is to be at work, and it literally means as represented by the revised version—the supplication of a righteous man avails much in its working. The literal meaning is stated something like this—this indicates a supplication that has an inward conformity to the mind of God. The effective fervent prayer is a prayer within you that is consistent with the mind of God. I think that is the bottom line as to how we can pray as effectively as Elijah. If you can pray with the mind of God, then you know your prayer is God's will and we can know we have the petition we ask for.

I want to look at the meaning of a righteous man. When we think of a righteous man, we think of a man who does not outwardly commit major sins. Truly, that is part of the meaning. The one who does whatever is right and just within itself and conforms himself to the revealed will of God, we would call this man a righteous man. He is one who has conditioned and conformed his life by the standards that are not his but God's. These are people who have a relationship with God and, as a result of this relationship, walk with Him. When you think of a righteous man, whom do you think of?

The word "avails" means it is capable of producing results, to be of force, to be of power. When I think of the prayer of a righteous man that avails much, I picture a person who does not live for himself but conforms his ways to the standards of God, not his own. Their focus is not on what someone else thinks of him; he wants to live up to the standard that God has for him. God's standard—that which is right, just, pure, and so forth. By holding to these standards, this person is more likely to know the will of God. He is walking with the Lord and is, to a degree, meshed with Him and walking in His ways and steps. Psalms 37:23 states that the steps of a good man are ordered by the Lord. Is the good man a righteous one?

If your prayer life doesn't produce the results you want, what is the reason? Psalms 66:18 says if I regard iniquity, the Lord will not hear me. There are three Scriptures we want to look at.

Proverbs 15:8 (NKJV)

8The sacrifice of the wicked is an abomination to the Lord, but the prayer of the upright is His delight.

1 Peter 3:12 (NKJV)

12For the eyes of the Lord are on the righteous, and His ears are open to their prayers; But the face of the Lord is against those who do evil.

Matthew 5:8 (NKJV)

⁸Blessed are the pure in heart, for they shall see God.

Remember, the word "pure" means not contaminated by sin, not mixed with anything else even if the other ingredient is pure within itself. So, you can have one pure ingredient here and another pure ingredient there, but if you mix the two, you contaminate them both. There is nothing wrong with either of them alone, both are pure, but if you put them together, they are contaminated. So then, pure means it is not mixed with anything.

Those who are pure in heart shall see God. Heart is the seat of the passions, feelings, affections, and impulses. Why, then, does our heart need to be pure? Because the Scripture says out of the heart precedes evil thoughts, murders, adulteries, and so on (Matthew 15:19).

To see God means more than just seeing God in the sweet by and by. Seeing God means to perceive God, to understand. You can read a Scripture 80,000 times, you can see it on the page, but you do not perceive the truth of it. Then one day, you are in prayer, reading that verse of Scripture, and you "see it." We have all had it happen to us. That is what it is talking about. You can see God working, you can see God moving in your church or your life, but to really perceive it is when it becomes alive to you. The pure in heart will perceive more about God.

We sometimes talk about the need for revival and how bad the world is. Let me ask you a question. Do you act as much like your Father as the lost do? A lost person is acting like his father. You cannot expect a lost person to change unless they get saved. They are just acting natural. Are we doing what is natural? With the Lord God Almighty within us, how natural is it for us to do some of the things we do? If it is not natural for Him to do it, then it should not be natural for us. We talk about how God understands when we do things contrary to His nature. I have heard people say of blatant sin, "God understands my needs and my feelings." He understands far more than we do and far more than we think He does, but He never excuses sin.

The Lord said if people come to the living water and drink, they will never thirst again. We are His representatives here on earth. Let me illustrate something to you. Take a glass of pure, clear water. Take a drink—good pure water. People should be able to drink from us. We say nobody is perfect, and I agree that nobody is perfect. But we say God understands that I have this thing in my life, and I really do not want to give this up. Here is what happens—we place a drop of contaminated water into our glass of pure, clean water. All it takes is one drop. You may not be able to tell the difference, but knowing this, who wants a drink? We think one little thing is not going to effect us— one little rotten thought, one little pet sin, one little thing—oh, it is no big deal, everybody does it. But we are a representative of the Living Water. If people drink from a contaminated fountain, they are going to get death and disease. It does not take but one drop to contaminate the entire fountain. It does not have to change colors; it can look the same on the outside. It might even taste the same. People may look at your life and not know the difference. If you have had a rotten thought, if you broke the law, if you had an affair with someone at work, they may not be able to see the difference by running into you at Wal-Mart. But you know the difference, and God knows the difference.

It is not usually all the big bad things that contaminate us so much, as it is all the little subtle things that trip us up. Because we are good Christian people, we are not going to the bar and getting drunk. But we might criticize someone, or talk about someone behind their back, or we might not forgive them from our heart, we might _____—fill in the blank. And those things contaminate us. Remember what Jesus said to the Pharisees, "You hypocrites, you clean up the outside where it looks wonderful, but the inside is full of dead men's bones." I want us to make sure our inside is not full of dead men's bones, because that is where God is looking, and that is where it is going to make a difference in our ability to pray with power. You may not commit what some consider the "big" sins, but you may do some of those other things I mentioned. I want you to realize that those still contaminate the Living Water.

Many years ago, again while in a Precept Bible study, I learned about the purity of salt. The Scripture says we are the salt of the earth, but if the salt loses its flavor, how shall it be seasoned? It is, therefore, good for nothing but to be thrown out and trampled underfoot by men (Matthew 5:13). May I tell you that salt never ever loses its effectiveness? You can leave it sitting on a shelf for 3,000 years, and it never loses its effectiveness. Then what is this Scripture talking about? In the Middle East, they mined salt from caves. In the caves was a substance that looked and felt like salt, but it was not salt. If while they were mining they either accidentally or intentionally mixed it with the salt, the salt was no longer pure salt. It was contaminated. The white substance looked like salt, but it was not salty. It had no effectiveness as a preservative or seasoning or making thirsty. The salt had lost its flavor, it had lost its saltiness, and it had lost its effectiveness, because there was too much of the other substance mixed in the salt. It was mixed with something that was not pure salt.

What about our lives? The Scripture says you are the salt of the earth. We are the people who make a difference. We are the people who have effectiveness. In two of the devotionals, we will talk about what salt does. Whether it is the water illustration or the salt illustration, I want us to think about how contaminated we are by the world's ways. I want us to think about how much of another substance is in the church, in our lives. I have a feeling if we removed worldliness from the church, we would not recognize the church. We presently do many things that could not be distinguished from the world. I don't mean any disrespect, and I know we have to change, but I get so aggravated when we think about how we have to entertain people to get people to come to church: we do not have to and should not do so. God's power is still God's power, and it is God's power that draws. It is not a rock band that will draw someone to God. Entertainment will not draw someone to God. People go to a bar to be entertained, but it doesn't draw them to Jesus. People go to a ball game to be entertained, but it does not draw them to Jesus. God's power is still powerful enough to draw people to Jesus.

Please hear me: I am not saying we need to do things like Grandpa did them, because his ways were probably messed up as well. But we have got to let God do His thing. The Scripture says if God be lifted up He will draw all men to Himself. That is what we must do. We have to love God, glorify God, lift Him up, praise Him, worship Him, and leave the rest to Him. Think about it: is your life contaminated with any other substance that looks like salt but is not pure salt? Is your life contaminated by some sin, whether considered big or small? Is there anything in your life that looks like Christianity but is only a well-made worldly likeness? Is your life contaminated with anything that resembles the right thing but is not exactly the way God intended, it has an element of the truth but lacks the substance of truth?

I think this subject is serious enough that we need to ask God to reveal any area where we need some decontamination. Let us ask Him if there are areas that need to be washed with the water of the Word until cleansing comes. The Scripture asks if you have lost your saltiness, what good are you. If you look like the world, dress as the world, talk like the world, and act like the world, you have lost your effectiveness, and what good are you? But don't despair. If this is where you are, run to the fountain for the cleansing flow and then return to your assignment of being salt to a lost world.

How do we have power in prayer?

- We need to be cleansed as Isaiah was cleansed. To see God's holiness and then to see our own sin and to allow God to cleanse us from that sin—then we can hear God's voice.

- We need to pray in Jesus's name, and I'm not talking about tagging His name onto the end of a prayer. You know that a name represents a person's character. To have power in prayer, we need to pray what Jesus would have prayed, to pray within His character (John 14:13–17). If it is not something Jesus would pray, neither should we pray that way. Jesus would never pray to hurt someone or that they get what they deserve. He will always pray redemptive prayers. Even for those people who horribly hurt us, we should never pray for God to give them what they deserve, because Jesus would pray for them to be brought to redemption. He would pray for mercy. We see His example as He hung on the cross and prayed for forgiveness for those who had just crucified Him. We need to pray within His character. We need to pray redemptive prayers.

- We need to pray in God's will and continually be filled with the Holy Spirit. To read 1 John. 5:14–15 is pretty powerful. It says, "This is the confidence we have, if we pray in His will we know He hears us and if He hears us we have what we ask for."

How do we pray in God's will? That is one of the most difficult things to understand. There is only way I know for sure to know God's will in praying, and that is found in Romans 8:26–27. This Scripture says the Spirit helps us pray in God's will. So then, how can we pray in the will of God? We ask the Holy Spirit to pray through us and for us.

This Scripture also teaches that we are to be filled continually with the Holy Spirit. Getting saved is a wonderful thing. And when we are saved, we receive the presence and power of the Holy Spirit within our lives. But the Scripture also teaches to be filled continuously with the Holy Spirit. This is an active thing, which is continuously happening. "Continually being filled with the Spirit of God" is how it is worded in the original language, if I understand correctly. If we are not continually being filled with the Holy Spirit, we are not as likely to know the will of God. It is okay to bow before God, tell Him you don't have a clue how to pray for a particular situation, and ask Him to pray through you. Ask Him to allow the Holy Spirit to pray though you and to show you His will. The Holy Spirit is the only One who actually knows the mind of God, the only One who knows God's will completely. As you align yourself with Him and allow the Holy Spirit to pray through you and speak to you, you may know God's will and then you know how to pray.

Sometimes there are no words. Have you ever been to a place in your prayer time or had a hurt so deep there were just no words to express the feelings? The Scripture says in those times that He can pray through us. The Holy Spirit makes intercession for us with words that are so deep our minds can't even get there. Our spirit groans with feelings too deep to be uttered. But He knows what we need, and He prays for us. What a wonderful mystery.

The strength of our prayer life and our power in prayer are related to the degree of our personal righteousness. Our personal righteousness is related to the degree to which we condition our lives to God's standards and rules rather than our own. The question is how much do we conform to or mesh with God? If we love Him, we will keep His commandments. As far as I can tell, His commandments are related to His standards. To keep the commandments as an attempt to keep the law and obtain righteousness results in a ping-pong game of pride verses despair. To align our lives with His in an expression of gratitude and outpouring of love which results in intimacy and a sense of beholding His face. Which do you want? Which sounds like it would produce real life? Which do you think would bring pleasure to the heart of God? Which do you think would produce power in prayer? Which do you think would produce joy in your prayer life?

How do we have power in prayer? How do we have joy in going before God in prayer? We are not to be contaminated with anything but be pure in heart. I don't think we will ever be totally pure, but the less contaminated we are, the more power and joy we have in prayer. I think it is probably on a continuum, and no, we won't be like God until we see Him, as the Scripture says, but the more we are in His presence, the more we perceive Him. The more we are in His Word, the more we perceive Him and the more we become like Him. I personally think that being in His presence is the key. I don't think you should lay down this book and go out and begin to try to clean up your life. If there is something in your life, I think you should begin to pray about it. If you want to be rid of it, tell Him you want to be righteous. I do not think you should use human effort alone to try to be righteous, because eventually you will fail. It is not by works of righteousness that we are saved (Titus 3:4–7).

I honestly believe with everything in me that the way we change and the way we become righteous is just being in His presence. I think that is the key to everything I know—everything—it's just being in His presence. Remember, the only thing He said for us to do is to love Him. When we love Him, everything else will fall into place. Love Him with all your heart, mind, body, soul, and strength, with everything that you are—and it will work.

RIGHTEOUSNESS: THE STRENGTH OF OUR PRAYERS

Devotionals

Righteousness: The Strength of Our Prayers

Who You Really Are Inside

Matthew 5:13 (NKJV)

¹³**"You are the salt of the earth; but if the salt loses its flavor, how shall it be seasoned? It is then good for nothing but to be thrown out and trampled underfoot by men."**

Salt is used to season food. It gives it flavor or added taste. Salt makes people thirsty. Salt preserves; it keeps food from spoiling or rotting. Jesus said that we are the salt of the earth. As long as we remain in this world, there is a preserving element. The world does not realize what a stabilizing factor we are. We should be putting some flavor of God into this present darkness.

If we eat a good deal of salt, we get very thirsty. We do not even have to realize the food is salty. It may taste fine, but there is salt within its contents. Once we are thirsty, we go to find water that will quench our thirst. Let me ask you a question. Does your life have enough salt to make those around you thirsty?

There is something very appealing about a person who genuinely loves the Lord. I am not talking about a person who just goes around saying, "Praise the Lord" all of the time. If a Christian is not authentic in devotion to the Lord, he tends to repel instead of draw others. You know the type of person that I am talking about.

On the other hand, those with an authentic devotion to God have a quality about them that draws others to them. I have heard people say of genuine Christians, "I would like to be like that person. They love God." Think about it: people were drawn to Jesus every day. He continuously had a crowd around Him. His inner qualities came out in His words, actions, and attitudes. What comes out of you?

Does enough of the Holy Spirit within you spill out each day so that people are drawn to you? We have talked before about acting like who you really are on the inside. Does it show? Are people around you thirsty because you are making them that way by your words, actions, and attitudes? People cannot manufacture the anointing of the Spirit of God on a life. Many try to, but anyone with discernment can tell the difference. Those who try to act holy and righteous only give the true follower of Jesus a bad name.

Prepare yourself as if you would literally stand or bow in His presence—you really are, though you can't see Him with your physical eyes.

- Determine that you are going to be "real."

- Determine that your life will be consistent with the inner qualities of the Holy Spirit within you.

- As you pray today, ask God to reveal your inner qualities to those around you. Please remember that the way inner qualities get revealed is by pushing your buttons. You find out what is really inside a person by someone shaking him up. You might be surprised as to what you find inside.

- Ask God to help you live in such a way as to make others thirsty for what you have.

- Ask God to allow you to point others to Living Water that can satisfy a deep thirst.

- Praise Him that He is so patient with us.

Righteousness: The Strength of Our Prayers

Contaminating Our Effectiveness

Today we will look at salt losing its flavor. I want you to apply this personally today. As a beginning point, let me remind you why salt loses its saltiness. Salt within itself never loses its flavor. The reason salt would lose its effectiveness is because it becomes contaminated with another substance that looks like salt. It has the same color, it has the same texture, but it is not salt.

I personally believe there are thousands of people within the church, as a whole, who act like Christians, talk like Christians, but are not Christians. They do not really know the Lord. Those people are enough to contaminate the church and render it somewhat ineffective. They present themselves as a part of the church. Unfortunately, the world looks at those who only have a resemblance to the real church and doesn't know the difference. Much of what we see today that represents the church does not at all look like the church Jesus established.

There are also those saved people who call Jesus Lord but are really their own masters. We all know some of them. They represent the church also. Their behavior contaminates the effectiveness of the church as well.

Then there are those people like us, those who want to be pleasing to the Lord. We are those who attend church every time the doors are open. In many cases, there is too much of the world's ways in our lives as well. We look too much like the world to be salty. The world has difficulty telling the difference between the church and themselves.

Today, I want you to think about your life. Consider your behavior, your words, and your attitudes. Are they pure salt, or are they mixed with something else? The more "other substances" that are within your life, the less effective the salt will be.

How much sugar would it take to conceal the taste of salt? I do not really know. Try it for yourself. The salt would still be there, but there would also be another white substance blended within. Since I have diabetes, I ran across a situation that illustrates this. I used to keep both sugar and salt in the same kind of container for canning purposes. When I looked in the container to get salt to can green beans, I could not determine if it was salt or sugar. They both were white; they both were granular. I had to taste them to determine the difference.

How many things in your life look like the world? How many attitudes feel like that of the world? How many words do you speak that are the same words the world speaks? There are even a lot of subtle ways we have contaminated the effectiveness of the church within the church walls. We often compromise the truth of God's Word to accommodate and draw people. The Holy Spirit and God's Word are still strong enough to reach the lost.

We do not need the world's ways to reach people. I am not saying that we should do everything like Grandpa did. His methods may have been mixed with his own ideas or beliefs. I am just saying that we need to be careful that we do not mix anything with the truth of the gospel.

Today as you pray:

- Ask God to reveal any way that you look like the world. Ask Him to reveal any way you dress like the world.

- Ask God to reveal any way you act like the world.

- Ask God to make you pure salt so that you can be effective in this world.

- Thank Him that His ways are good and righteous.

- Pray for your church that they would never adopt anything that contaminates the truth.

- Ask Him to show you how to be purely what He wants.

Righteousness: The Strength of Our Prayers

Our Own Holiness

Isaiah 6:1–8

¹In the year that King Uzziah died, I saw the Lord sitting on a throne, high and lifted up, and the train of His *robe* filled the temple. ²Above it stood seraphim; each one had six wings; with two he covered his face, with two he covered his feet, and with two he flew. ³And one cried to another and said: "Holy, holy, holy *is* the LORD of hosts; the whole earth *is* full of His glory!" ⁴And the posts of the door were shaken by the voice of him who cried out, and the house was filled with smoke. ⁵So I said: "Woe is me, for I am undone! Because I *am* a man of unclean lips, and I dwell in the midst of a people of unclean lips; for my eyes have seen the King, the LORD of hosts." ⁶Then one of the seraphim flew to me, having in his hand a live coal *which* he had taken with the tongs from the altar.

Today we want to look at our own holiness. We will review as we notice that Isaiah saw and acknowledged God's holiness before he was able to recognize his own condition. Read the Scripture carefully and see if you catch that. I believe he specifically names his sin when he said, "Because I am a man of unclean lips." Only after he saw the holiness of the Lord was he able to see his own clearly and only then clearly see other sin. We cannot clearly judge another's sin without first examining ourselves. When I see the magnitude of my own sin, the sin of another is not so significant. Isaiah did not point his finger at others. He considered himself dwelling among a sinful people. He recognized that he was not any better than they at being holy. He saw God high and lifted up; he saw God's holiness. Then he saw his own true state. I wonder what we would do and feel if we were to see the true holiness of God.

Once he acknowledged his sinful condition, the seraphim came to him, having a live coal of fire taken from the tongs of the altar. With that, Isaiah's sin was purged. He was then able to hear the call of the Lord. When Isaiah said he was a man of unclean lips, he was saying that his language was not pleasing to God. The lips are gateways to honesty or deception. The language of God's people should be rejoicing, prayerful, filled with God's Word, truthful, wise, righteous, and without sin.

There are several ways one's language can be displeasing to God. We may show a direct disregard for God and His ways through the use of foul language. Sometimes we say things toward other people that also show dishonesty or disregard. We may have a problem with gossip or slander. Only you know the things that you say in your heart—and those that proceed from your mouth.

Christians should be saying the same things that our Father is saying. We should be blessing and not cursing. We should be praising not complaining. You get the picture.

Today, as you prepare to pray, sit quietly before the Lord and allow the light of the Holy Spirit shine into your heart.

- Seek to see the Lord high and lifted up.

- Ask to see His holiness more clearly.

- Sit in His presence, and as you behold Him, ask Him to expose you to the light of His presence. Look at yourself honestly: is your language pleasing to the Lord?

- Ask the Lord to cleanse any area He shows you as a problem area in your life.

- Ask that the Lord cleanse your lips. This includes any vain thing that escapes your lips, whether directly degrading to the Lord's purpose or just some vain useless way of speech. It could be gossip or criticism.

- Ask Him to place upon your lips words of praise and glory.

Please read the following passages of Scripture:

- Job 8:21
- Psalms 17:1
- Psalms 119:13
- Proverbs 12:19
- Proverbs 14:7; 15:7
- Proverbs 16:13
- Job 2:10

Righteousness: The Strength of Our Prayers

Here Am I, Send Me

After Isaiah was cleansed, he was able to hear the voice of the Lord. The voice of the Lord was saying, "Whom shall I send, and who will go for us?" Some believe the voice of the Lord is always speaking, but we rarely are in a condition to hear Him. I really do not know; I just know that once Isaiah's perspective changed and the sin cleared, he heard.

God was expressing a desire for someone to be of service to Him. There was a need. Who would be willing to fill that need? Isaiah responded by saying, "Here am I, send me." Sometimes people do not really want to hear a call from God, because you must respond once you hear His voice. You must say yes or no, or try to avoid the question all together. I think many would rather avoid His voice, because they do not want to deal with the question. Whether you choose to hear the call, you will still be held accountable for the purpose God planned for your life.

Many think they are not capable of doing what God calls them to do. When you think about that, we are saying that we know more than God does. What a lack of trust. If He calls us, He equips us to do whatever He calls us to do. He has promised to go with us. What are we really saying to the God who formed us when we say, "I can't"? Is that the clay rebuking the potter? There is something wrong with that picture, don't you think?

Today as you pray:

- Ask God to cleanse you inside and out.

- Ask to hear His call. Tell Him you are willing to hear, but only if you really are.

- Pray that you will be willing to respond as Isaiah, "Here am I, Lord send me." It may be many small steps the Lord asks you to take in your life. It could be anything from cooking a pot of homemade chicken noodle soup to giving a child a hug. Do not be afraid to hear Him. He may not ask you to travel to Africa, then again, He might. Trust Him.

- Praise Him that He made you, saved you, and gave you the Holy Spirit. Praise Him that you can hear Him.

Day 5 Devotional

Righteousness: The Strength of Our Prayers

Abiding in Him

1 John 3:24 (NKJV)

²⁴Now he who keeps His commandments abides in Him, and He in him. And by this we know that He abides in us, by the Spirit whom He has given us.

John 15:4, 7, 10 (NKJV)

⁴Abide in Me, and I in you. As the branch cannot bear fruit of itself, unless it abides in the vine, neither can you, unless you abide in Me. ⁷If you abide in Me, and My words abide in you, you will ask what you desire, and it shall be done for you. ¹⁰If you keep My commandments, you will abide in My love, just as I have kept My Father's commandments and abide in His love.

Notice that in two of these references, abiding is linked with obeying His commands. There also seems to be a connection between those things and abiding in His love. Verse 7 says that if we abide in Him and His words abide in us, we can ask whatever we wish and it will be done for us. That is a powerful statement.

So how can we abide in Him? Abide is also translated in some passages as continue. When I think of the word continue, I think of consistent or perhaps staying in one place. For most of us, our prayer lives are so inconsistent that it is pitiful. We are hot one day and cold the next day. As a matter of fact, for many of us, our whole lives of service to God are inconsistent. Very seldom do we see a Christian who continues in service without interruption.

Abide means to remain or dwell in a place. In John's writing, it is referring to the relation where one person stands with another, to be united with the other in heart, mind, and will. Read this definition slowly. Do you fit the definition? Are you united with Him in heart, mind, and will? Do you remain in that state of being? The promise is if we do, whatever we ask will be done for us. If we remained united with Him, whatever we ask would also be His will, His heart, and His mind about the matter.

If God's teachings and the things He says are true and remain and continue in us, whatever we purpose, intend, or have in mind will be done for us. I think that is a picture of being one with Him. Jesus prayed that we would be one with Him and the Father. If we keep His commands, we abide. This means that we remain, continue, or dwell in His love. That is a place I would like to live for a very long time.

As always, prepare yourself for a time with God. Today as you pray:

- Examine your own life and heart to determine how closely you keep His commands.

- Ask the Lord to make it clear each time you stray from His commands.

- Pray that God will give you a love for His commands and a desire to obey them at all costs.

- Ask the Lord to help you abide with Him. To be united in mind, heart, and will with the Lord. Take each aspect and separately pray about each area of your being.

- Ask Him to teach you to abide in Him and bear much fruit. If a branch does not produce fruit, it is lifted up and tied to keep it from getting back down in the dirt and mud. If you have fallen down into the dirt and have become ineffective at producing, ask Him to lift you up and clean you off so that you once again can produce fruit. Remember, a branch just abides while the sap running through it actually produces fruit, just as we abide while the Holy Spirit flows through us to produce much fruit for the kingdom of God.

CHAPTER 10

Worship: The Completion of Our Prayers

Matthew 6:9–13 (NKJV)

⁹**In this manner, therefore, pray: Our Father in heaven, hallowed be Your name. ¹⁰Your kingdom come. Your will be done on earth *as it is* in heaven. ¹¹Give us this day our daily bread. ¹²And forgive us our debts, as we forgive our debtors. ¹³And do not lead us into temptation, but deliver us from the evil one. For Yours is the kingdom and the power and the glory forever. Amen.**

For Yours is the kingdom and the power and the glory forever. Notice the model prayer begins with hallowing His name and ends with acknowledging His rule and His majesty. First, His dominion is acknowledged, that is, His right to reign in a believer's heart. Do you daily acknowledge His right to reign in your heart—the very core of your emotions, your motives, and your thoughts? To have intimacy with Him, to have a joyful prayer life, to have an effective prayer life, He must be free to reign in your heart. Out of the heart proceed the issues of life. Will you yield your heart to His rule?

Next, His power is recognized. The word here is "Dunamis," which is where we get our word for dynamite. The word means to be able.

May I ask you to consider what Jesus was able to do while in human form, walking in this world? Does not the Scripture say He is the same yesterday, today, and forever (Hebrews 13:8)? May I also suggest that He is able to do exceedingly abundantly above all that we might ask or think, according to the power that works in us (Ephesians 3:20). We have not seen the full power of God demonstrated; our minds can't comprehend the magnitude of His power.

The third part of the verse says the glory belongs to Him. What does glory mean? According to *The Complete Word Study Dictionary*, the word for glory means to think or recognize. I love what this dictionary says about glory; let me quote it.

> **Etymologically, the word primarily means thought or opinion, and thus in a secondary sense reputation, praise, honor (true or false), splendor, light, perfection, rewards, (temporal and eternal). Thus the doxa (glory) of man is human opinion and is shifty, uncertain, and often based on error, and its pursuit for its own safety in unworthy. But there is a glory of God which must be absolute and changeless. God's opinion marks the true value of things as they appear to the eternal mind, and God's favorable opinion is true glory. Giving glory to God is ascribing to Him His full recognition. The glory of man, on the other hand, is the ideal condition in which God created man. (p. 478, #1391)**

I love the part of this definition that says that human opinion is shifty and uncertain. That is such a true statement. Human opinion changes with the wind. My opinion of myself changes with such things as the amount of sleep I've had the night before. Human opinion cannot be trusted.

I want to bring out two aspects to think about concerning the above verse. Glory is thought or opinion, and we know human opinion depends on our circumstances and feelings, so human opinion cannot be trusted—right? We also know that God's thoughts and opinions are absolutely correct, so His opinions and thoughts of us are absolutely correct—right? What does He say about us? For starters, we are accepted in the Beloved (Ephesians 1:6). I challenge you to search the Scriptures to see what they say about God's thoughts of us—begin with Jeremiah 29:11.

I wonder if we could say for Yours is the glory—thoughts and opinions of me are correct, mine are not. Could we say that God's thoughts and opinions of my worth are correct, mine are not? Could we say that God's thoughts and opinions are correct of—you name the situation, circumstance, or person—and mine are not?

Another way to think about giving God glory is for you and me to have the correct thoughts and opinions of God. To give Him glory is to recognize and acknowledge Him for who He truly is and to express His worth in worship. We are to ascribe to Him, as fully as is possible, His true recognition. To give Him glory is to say, "Lord, you reign over all. You are able to do whatever You want, and I honor You. I recognize You as King of Kings and Lord of Lords."

Jesus began this teaching on prayer with "Hallowed be Thy name." That was recognition of His holiness. By beginning with this, He showed us that we are to honor His name. He then taught to seek God for particular things. At the end again, He taught us to recognize His greatness.

The last phrase in this passage of Scripture from Matthew 6 establishes these facts. It establishes who is in control. It establishes who is King. It establishes that He is capable. He gets all the recognition and honor. Everything is fully ascribed to Him.

Once we have prayed, we need to recognize that He is the only one who is able to perform what we have asked. His kingdom is good and right. He is God; He did not have to be good, but He is. He is Lord over all things. He is Lord over creation, health, emotions, demons, and all things are in submission to Him.

We thank Him for His glory. We give Him glory for establishing a relationship with us so that we could pray to Him. We give Him glory for hearing our prayer. For being powerful enough to accomplish what He wants. We give Him glory that His will is always good. That He has compassion and mercy on us to give us only those things that are best for us. We honor Him for the answer, whatever it might be.

1 Chronicles 16:29 (NKJV)

²⁹**Give to the LORD the glory** *due* **His name; bring an offering, and come before Him. Oh, worship the LORD in the beauty of holiness!**

What is worship anyway? We are commanded to do it in Scripture. I cannot define worship in a sentence or two; actually, I can't define it all. It is praise, but it is more than praise. Some teach that thanksgiving is given for what He has done and praise is given for who He is. Worship may be expressed through praise and thanksgiving or by deeds done in acknowledgment of His Lordship. Worship can take many forms, such as, bowing, singing, serving, lifting hands; there are really too many expressions to mention. Worship is a matter of the heart. The same things just mentioned can be done and not be worship of God.

Worship is described in *The Complete Word Study Dictionary* as, "to kiss toward." This definition makes a lot of sense when you understand in that culture, when two equals greeted one another, they kissed on the lips. Two people of somewhat less-equal standing were expected to kiss on the cheek. But when one person was greatly inferior to the other, the lesser would bow on his knees with his forehead to the ground and kiss toward the one of higher authority. To worship Him is to realize His authority and place over us and show our deference to Him. Any act we do to convey our attitude of heart is worship to Him.

To worship requires at least three elements. Worship involves reverence. This includes the honor and respect directed toward the Lord in thought and feeling. It is a willful committing of oneself to His deity. Worship includes public expression. Worship can also mean service. It presents a picture of slaves serving a master. Worship especially involves the joyful service of Christians. It is a life of obedience to God.

John 4:24 (NKJV)

²⁴**God** *is* **Spirit, and those who worship Him must worship in spirit and truth.**

What does this mean to worship him in spirit and truth? Our spirit is the part that is made alive at salvation. It is that inner part that communicates with invisible God. Man's spirit is indwelt by God's Spirit; they become one. The Holy Spirit enables or helps us to communicate with God; therefore, the Holy Spirit helps us worship God. The outward expression is displayed both in praise and service.

Genesis 22:1–18 (NKJV)

[1]Now it came to pass after these things that God tested Abraham, and said to him, "Abraham!" And he said, "Here I am." [2]Then He said, "Take now your son, your only *son* Isaac, whom you love, and go to the land of Moriah, and offer him there as a burnt offering on one of the mountains of which I shall tell you." [3]So Abraham rose early in the morning and saddled his donkey, and took two of his young men with him, and Isaac his son; and he split the wood for the burnt offering, and arose and went to the place of which God had told him. [4]Then on the third day Abraham lifted his eyes and saw the place afar off. [5]And Abraham said to his young men, "Stay here with the donkey; the lad and I will go yonder and worship, and we will come back to you." [6]So Abraham took the wood of the burnt offering, and laid *it* on Isaac his son; and he took the fire in his hand, and a knife, and the two of them went together. [7]But Isaac spoke to Abraham his father and said, "My father!" And he said, "Here I am, my son." Then he said, "Look, the fire and the wood, but where *is* the lamb for a burnt offering?" [8]And Abraham said, "My son, God will provide for Himself the lamb for a burnt offering." So the two of them went together. [9]Then they came to the place of which God had told him. And Abraham built an altar there and placed the wood in order; and he bound Isaac his son and laid him on the altar, upon the wood. [10]And Abraham stretched out his hand and took the knife to slay his son. [11]But the Angel of the LORD called to him from heaven and said, "Abraham, Abraham!" So he said, "Here I am." [12]And He said, "Do not lay your hand on the lad, or do anything to him'; for now I know that you fear God, since you have not withheld your son, your only *son,* from Me." [13]Then Abraham lifted his eyes and looked, and there behind *him was* a ram caught in a thicket by its horns. So Abraham went and took the ram, and offered it up for a burnt offering instead of his son. [14]And Abraham

called the name of he place, The-LORD-Will-Provide; as it is said *to* this day, in the Mount of the LORD it shall be provided. [15]Then the Angel of the LORD called to Abraham a second time out of heaven, [16]and said: "By Myself I have sworn, says the LORD, because you have done this thing, and have not withheld your son, your only *son*—[17] blessing I will bless you, and multiplying I will multiply your descendants as the stars of the heaven and as the sand which *is* on the seashore; and your descendants shall possess the gate of their enemies. [18]In you seed all the nations of the earth shall be blessed, because you have obeyed My voice."

Notice verse 5: this is the first time this Hebrew word is translated worship. The word "bowed" is used in Genesis 18:2 and Genesis 19:1. This is the first mention of the word "worship" in the Bible. According to this Scripture, what is involved in worship? Worship is a test of your love. Worship is a test of your heart's devotion. Worship is a test of obedience. Worship is a test of faith.

What did Abraham lay on the altar of worship? He laid the covenant promise on the altar. God had given it, and it was God who would keep it and perform it. He laid the future on the altar. He laid his greatest love and possession on the altar. He laid his compete trust on the altar. Abraham was laying himself on the altar, not just Isaac.

He was laying his total life out for God to take in any way that He chose. This was a total surrender of Abraham's ideas, hopes, and feelings. It was a total surrender of his will to God's will. We are told to worship in spirit and in truth. Abraham worshipped in spirit when he was willing to believe and trust God's Word. When he laid all that was within him on the altar, he was worshipping God. He worshipped in truth when he took the wood and laid Isaac upon it and drew back the knife to kill him.

To worship in spirit comes from within. It is a heart thing. To worship in truth is the outward expression of that which is within; it is the obedience part. Worship is not coming to church. Worship is not sitting in church. Worship is not singing in church. Worship is not listening in church. Worship is not just service, visiting, praying, and so forth. It can be all those things, but without the intent of the heart, these things are nothing more than activities to impress God or someone else. Worship happens when you have completely yielded to God, and you want to please and give to Him. When we stand before Him in praise and become one with Him in mind, will, and emotion, we worship.

When we are in God's presence and He has filled us, we lose a sense of self. He is all in all. We lose a degree of physical awareness. We are more aware of Him. We want what He wants. We want to please Him; we love Him. We see things differently. We see more through His heart.

It is a wonderful experience to stand in His presence. It is a wonderful experience to present our offering to the living God and feel His pleasure. But, it is a difficult thing to come to the point where Abraham came. He lay down everything in total surrender of heart and life. The pouring out of your total self for God alone to scoop up and use is a difficult thing to do. Did you notice verse 17? It was only after Abraham's obedience that God said, "I will greatly bless you."

You can hear God's pleasure at Abraham's offering and obedience. Are you ready to surrender totally that which you love the most? Are you ready to surrender your future? Are you ready to surrender your hope? Are you ready to surrender your trust? Are you ready to completely offer yourself as a burnt offering, wholly consumed, signifying the total dedication of your heart and life in spirit and in truth?

WORSHIP: THE COMPLETION OF OUR PRAYERS

Devotionals

Worship: The Completion of Our Prayers

Love Him Completely

Matthew 22:37–38 (NKJV)

[37]Jesus said to him, "'You *shall love the LORD your God with all your heart, with all your soul, and with all your mind.'* This is *the* first and great commandment."

To love God is the foundation of worship. It is the motivating factor in true worship. Love involves feelings, and I am certainly glad it does. But the primary meaning of real love is to make a deliberate choice to act for the welfare of someone else. Love is seen through actions. The Scripture says if we love the Lord, we will keep His commandments, and that requires action on our part (John 14:15). We could tell our children we love them till the cows come home, but if we did not feed them or nurture them, our words would be empty. Love is expressed by actions not feelings.

Today, I want you to examine yourself in light of this Scripture. Do you love the Lord your God with all your heart, soul, mind, and strength? First, is He your Master? Do you esteem Him as such? Is there any part of yourself that you refuse to submit to His Lordship?

Are all your desires given to Him? Are your affections for "things" submitted to Him? Are all your feelings under His authority? Are passions and impulses yours or His? Is He the center of your life? If He isn't, who is? Maybe it is you. Are your thoughts turned toward Him? Is your intellectual ability and potential submitted to His Lordship? Is your every breath breathed for His benefit and purpose? Will you give your last breath for Him? Are you willing to give your physical strength for His use? Is your own health for His glory or yours?

Think about each of these questions. Meditate on them and then ask God to examine your heart. Submit each of these areas to your Lord God Almighty. Ask Him to cause you to love Him in all of these ways and more. Bow before Him in reverence and honor. Worship Him in the beauty of holiness. He is worthy of our greatest love.

Be blessed!

Worship: The Completion of Our Prayers

Worship Him Alone

Matthew 15:1–9 (NKJV)

¹Then the scribes and Pharisees who were from Jerusalem came to Jesus, saying, ²"Why do Your disciples transgress the tradition of the elders? For they do not wash their hands when they eat bread?" ³He answered and said to them, "Why do you also transgress the commandment of God because of you tradition? ⁴For God commanded, saying, *'Honor your father and your mother'*; and *'He who curses father or mother, let him be put to death.'* ⁵But you say, 'Whoever says to his father or mother, "Whatever profit you might have received from me *is* a gift *to God*"—*⁶*then he need not honor his father or mother.' Thus you have made the commandment of God of no effect by your tradition. ⁷Hypocrites! Well did Isaiah prophesy about you, saying: *⁸These people draw near to me with their mouth, and honor Me with their lips, but their heart is far from Me. ⁹And in vain they worship Me, teaching as doctrines the commandments of men.'"*

Mark 7:1–13 (NKJV)

¹Then the Pharisees and some of the scribes came together to Him, having come from Jerusalem. ²Now when they saw some of His disciples eat bread with defiled, that is, with unwashed hands, they found fault. ³For the Pharisees and all the Jews do not eat unless they wash *their* hands in a special way, holding the tradition of the elders. ⁴*When they come* from the marketplace, they do not eat unless they wash. And there are many other things which they have received and hold, *like* the washing of cups, pitchers, copper vessels, and couches. ⁵Then the Pharisees and scribes asked Him, "Why do Your disciples

not walk according to the tradition of the elders, but eat bread with unwashed hands?" ⁶He answered and said to them, "Well did Isaiah prophesy of you hypocrites, as it is written: 'This people honors Me with their lips, but their heart is far from Me. ⁷And in vain they worship Me, teaching as doctrines the commandments of men.' ⁸For laying aside the commandment of God, you hold the tradition of men—the washing of pitchers and cups, and many other such things you do." ⁹He said to them, "All too well you reject the commandment of God, that you may keep your tradition." ¹⁰For Moses said, 'Honor your father and your mother', and, 'He who curses father or mother, let him be put to death.' ¹¹But you say, 'If a man says to his father or mother, "Whatever profit you might have received from me is Corban"—'(that is, a gift to God), ¹²then you no longer let him do anything for his father or his mother, ¹³making the word of God of no effect through your tradition which you have handed down. And many such things you do."

How much of what we do and call worship is really tradition of men? I am not at all saying that traditions are bad. They become wrong when we put them above or in place of our relationship with God. When we listen to and obey what is expected of us rather than listen to the voice of the Holy Spirit, we are listening to the wrong voices. Think about how we conduct church services. Which parts are tradition and which are directed by biblical doctrine? How much of our worship flows out of our life in Him? Is the River of Life flowing out of us spilling onto those around us? What are we bringing to offer in worship during each service?

Personally, I would like to see the church as a whole get away from the traditional two songs, a prayer, an offering, ten more minutes of music, and then a sermon. What would you like to see happen in your worship services? How would they be conducted? What part would you be willing to play?

Today as you pray:

- Ask God to reveal any tradition of men you hold in higher esteem than Him.

- Ask Him to show you, or us as a church, how He would like to see the worship services conducted.

- Ask God to lead your church into a freedom to worship. Not to be out of order or to have chaos, but to have Him hold the order of service.

- Ask God to free you to worship Him in a way that would not offend your brother but that would be pleasing unto Him.

- Ask Him to show you how to express your love for Him in a way that makes Him smile.

Worship: The Completion of Our Prayers

Bow Down Before God

Revelation 11:16–18 (NKJV)

¹⁶And the twenty-four elders who sat before God on their thrones fell on their faces and worshiped God, ¹⁷saying: "We give You thanks, O Lord God Almighty, the One who is and who was and who is to come, because You have taken Your great power and reigned. ¹⁸The nations were angry, and Your wrath has come, and the time of the dead, that they should be judged, and that You should reward Your servants the prophets and the saints, and those who fear Your name, small and great, and should destroy those who destroy the earth."

Today, we want to think about part of the definition of worship. Part of the definition means to bow down, to prostrate oneself. Many of you have never been in this position before the Lord. Hear me: I am not saying you must prostrate yourself before God to be heard. I would like for you to have the experience though.

Before you lie down with your face to the floor, please kneel before the Lord and ask His presence and His blessing in this adventure. I do hope it will be an adventure for you. Ask the Lord to fill you with His presence and help you see Him high and lifted up, as Isaiah did. Ask Him to bring you to the place where you are compelled to bow yourself as completely as possible. Envision the Lord before you; what would you do?

As you begin to sense God's presence, open your Bibles to Revelation 11:16–18. There on the floor before God, begin to worship Him by reading and praying this passage of Scripture to Him. Repeat this Scripture as your prayer. Then, elaborate on it. Thank Him for specific things He has done in your life. Thank Him that He reigns and will reward those who fear His name. Do you fear His name? Get an early start on what is going to be taking place in heaven. Why not do it right now?

Worship: The Completion of Our Prayers

Worship in Truth

John 4:23 (NKJV)

²³But the hour is coming, and now is, when the true worshipers will worship the Father in spirit and truth; for the Father is seeking such to worship Him.

The Lord is seeking those who will worship Him in spirit and in truth. Is the Lord seeking you to worship Him? We have already discussed what it means to worship in spirit and truth. If you need to refresh yourself, go back and read chapter 10.

By this time, you know how to prepare yourself for prayer. Do so now.

- Tell God you really want to know how to worship.

- Ask Him to personally teach you.

- Ask Him to let you stand in His presence so completely that there is nothing else but Him. To be aware only of His presence is our goal. I really believe that is where He wants us to be. I think if you sincerely ask, He will grant it to you. Spend some time in worship today. Just bask in His love for you for a while.

After you have done business with the King:

- Ask Him to show you how to worship Him in truth.

- Ask, "What is it that I can do to live out what I offer you on the inside? In what way can I serve You today? Speak Lord, for Your servant listens."

- Listen very closely for His voice.

- Are you willing to hear Him?

- Are you willing to obey Him? Ask with sincerity, "Lord, what can I do this day to make you smile?"

Oh, precious one, whatever He says, please obey! Worship Him in truth today! Make Him smile! Bless you!

Day 5 Devotional

Worship: The Completion of Our Prayers

Review

Psalms 105:1–6 (NKJV)

¹Oh, give thanks to the LORD! Call upon His name; make known His deeds among the peoples! ²Sing to Him, sing psalms to Him; talk of all His wondrous works! ³Glory in His holy name; let the hearts of those rejoice who seek the LORD! ⁴Seek the LORD and His strength; seek His face evermore! ⁵Remember His marvelous works which He has done, His wonders, and the judgments of His mouth, ⁶O seed of Abraham His servant, You children of Jacob, His chosen ones!

1 Chronicles 16:29 (NKJV)

²⁹Give to the LORD the glory *due* His name; bring an offering, and come before Him. Oh, worship the LORD in the beauty of holiness!

Today, I want you to review the ten principles of prayer that we have studied. List each principle, and use this last day to list anything God has taught you related to each lesson.

- List anything that He revealed to you through the chapters or the daily devotionals.

- Record anything that He spoke to you specifically or any time of special blessing. Ask Him to bring those times to your remembrance. Write them down as they come to your mind.

- Thank Him for each item on your list, each word, each blessing. He is so very good. He has given to you. Now it is time to give back.

- Bring Him an offering of thanksgiving! Come before Him and worship Him! Give Him the glory due His name!

When you have finished giving Him glory, would you please pray for me? Would you please pray that God gives me favor? Would you please pray that God anoint the words of this book? My prayer has always been that He would bless, break, and multiply it to feed thousands.

Then, would you please pray for each person who will read this book? Ask God to direct you in praying for them. Please pray for their prayer lives and their walk with the Lord. Pray that each one will know a new level of intimacy with God.

Thank you so very much for joining me in this journey. I will always be thankful for you. I pray God richly blesses you for your participation.

Much love,

Connie Hubbard